PRAISES FOR UNCLUTTERED
AND LISA GIESLER

This book was very riveting, as Lisa candidly shared her personal life experiences and those of others. She clearly demonstrated that regardless of the challenges one may face, it is never beyond the reach of the human soul to help others in need. As we stretch beyond ourselves. In our pursuit to help others, we find the help we receive is far greater than that which we give.

Lisa's stories show that the road of life brings many experiences and an array of people along our paths. Although there is no perfect life, life is what we make of it! Answered prayers sometime come in the most unexpected ways, shapes, and forms. It is not where we start, but how we finish the race that matters most. Though we may not have control over every event that comes our way, we can have control over our response and ultimately the effect the event has on us, as Lisa so explicitly shares.

Lisa's compassion is contagious as she brings the realization that each person has a story to tell, that we should not be so quick to pass judgment, and that we never know what someone is going through.

Although this book is easy reading, it is one which is very difficult to put down. Thank you, Lisa, for being vulnerable and sharing your heart. I believe this will aid you in your recovery and help numerous others, as well. God bless you for your honesty!

Cathy Cilluffo, Pastor
Believer's Life Family Church
New Orleans, LA

Uncluttered takes an insightful look beyond the clutter and chaos of our lives and reveals how it directly relates to experiences and challenges we have or have had. It is a refreshingly candid and down-to-earth story of Lisa's life, intermingled with stories of her clients that are both entertaining, poignant, and designed to make us realize that the things we collect, both physical and emotional, memories and messes, all work together to keep us from our purpose in this life. If you're looking for a way out of your mess, you'll find a roadmap in the pages of this book.

Carol Jones
Editor-in-Chief
Lucid Books

Lisa leads her reader through a very personal journey of her life and at the same time add humor and reality to life's lemons! Unclutter is an easy read yet chilling on many levels. Lisa describes hell and back and how it gave her purpose in helping others.

Linda Brown
LLB Traditional Design
Houston, TX

Lisa Giesler has a personality bigger than Texas and her charming personality is "flavored" with her native New Orleans "accent", but her true magnetism comes from her authentic love for people. I seriously doubt Lisa has ever met a stranger who didn't walk away with a new title of "friend."

Keri Ann Reardon
Owner/Artist Makeup by Keri Ann
Houston, TX

Lisa is a breath of fresh air and brings energy to every project. I appreciate her drive and determination. We need more like her.

Jacquie Baly
Policy Analyst, FOX26
President, BalyProjects

Lisa is such a wealth of resource for organizing your home and office. Her solutions work and make total sense. I've put to use many of her ideas and shared them with my friends. With her energy and sweet, lively personality she will always surprise you with how much she knows and how much she shares. She has such a generous nature.

Christina Hawkins
GlobalSpex Internet Marketing

She's just a bundle of joy and energy. It's a pleasure to work with someone who has found her gift and obviously loves what she does.

Staci Holtzman

As a speaker, she has shared her gift with women throughout the community. The ability to captivate and motivate her audience is one of her most valuable assets. What separates Lisa from others is her ability to relate to women from all walks of life.

Tazarra Berrien
Makeover 101 Ministry Leader

Lisa is awesome. She has a truly kind and caring heart. Thankful for all she has done!

Lisa Krumm Anhaiser
LBL Event Rentals, LLC
Houston, TX

She's so enthusiastic about what she is doing and her ability and desire to help people is always at the forefront. I marvel at her everlasting energy.

Debbie Marcell
Gary Greene Realtors
Sugar Land, TX

UNCLUTTERED

UNCLUTTERED

Discovering Strength and
Purpose in the Chaos of Life

LISA GIESLER

LUCIDBOOKS

Uncluttered: Discovering Strength and Purpose in the Chaos of Life
© Lisa Giesler

Published by Lucid Books in Houston, TX.
www.LucidBooks.net

ISBN-13: 978-1-63296-027-6
ISBN-10: 1632960273

Special Sales: Most Lucid Books titles are available in special quantity discounts. Custom imprinting or excerpting can also be done to fit special needs. Contact Lucid Books at info@lucidbooks.net.

FOREWORD

"Uncluttered" is a compelling read with an important message: understanding how to gain and maintain peace and happiness through the clutter in our lives. In the hustle and bustle of life, we tend to lose focus of what is truly important and what makes us not only happy, but at peace. This book guides you through your clutter to face your personal truth! Lisa Giesler has the ability to "hit a nerve" as she unravels the very core of who we are at heart. Giesler conveys through stories that are hilarious and painful to strike her audience attention to their personal struggles with physical clutter. This book explains how living in clutter expresses our innermost emotions. As a Motivational and Empowerment speaker, it is obvious that some people cannot get to the next level due to their past which hinders their personal growth. Giesler's book helps individuals to live to their potential once they face their clutter. "Uncluttered" will give insight to readers on how to make peace with their past to gain their potential with organization.

Sonya M. Sloan, M.D.
Orthopedic Surgeon
ME&WE Inc., Founder
First Lady of The Luke Church

This book is dedicated to the memory of Sally Turpin,
Professional Organizer 11/15/1963 – 4/24/2014

When I felt God was guiding me to become an organizer,
it was her mom who said "Sally's an organizer".
Aside from God, she was the motivation for starting
A Time and Place for Everything, LLC.
Sally was my first business mentor.

ACKNOWLEDGEMENTS

To my husband, Joseph, my steady rock

To my sister, Judy, my prayer warrior

To my son, Joe, thank you for your humor, energy, and your willingness to help

To my son, Charlie, you helped to co-write this book, thank you for your wisdom and patience

To my friend, Lisa Krumm Anhaiser, thank you for holding my hand through this journey and coffee

To my editor, Carol Jones, you are the best, thank you for helping to lighten a very heavy story

To Renee' Clark and the women of Triumph Church, thank you for your text messages and all the support during a very difficult time

To all of my friends, too numerous to include, I couldn't have done this without you, thank you, I am so blessed

To my business coach, Mark Ehrlich, true, the mentor at times was the tormentor, but I did it

no regrets. lessons learned. strength gained.
my faith has kept me.
~Lisa Giesler

CONTENTS

PROLOGUE:
SOME COMMON GROUND

I have a phrase I often use in life. I say, "No Regrets, Lessons Learned, Strength Gained, My Faith Has Kept Me"

As I go through life, I aim to live it to the fullest, with no regrets. Yes, absolutely I make mistakes along the way, we all do. But it is through my mistakes (and the mistakes of others) that I learn my most valuable lessons, and through those lessons that I gain strength. And in the days when the chaos and clutter of my own life threaten to overtake me, I remember that God has given me a purpose on this earth, to help others discover the strength and purpose in their own lives.

I wrote this book to break down some walls, open some doors, and shed some light on what causes us to become bogged down in the chaos and clutter of our lives.

It's easy to look at other people and believe their lives are as pretty on the inside as they are on the outside. In fact, I think society and social media would have us believe we MUST live pretty, perfect lives to be normal, but that simply isn't true. In my many years as a professional organizer, I have come to realize that a messy home is often an indicator that there is more going on in someone's life than just a busy schedule and a cluttered living space. Many of my clients, with seemingly successful lives, are dealing with difficult life issues, some living in abusive situations, and many hiding from past hurts.

Now, as I sit with my clients, I know to truly help them, I must be concerned with the bigger picture, not just what I can see on the surface, but what is hidden under the clutter and chaos of their lives. I know it is huge for them to admit they need help and allow me into their worlds. So, patiently and sometimes painfully, I listen as they explain why the messes in their homes and businesses have occurred. And as they talk about their clutter and chaos, when they feel like they can trust me, they open up and share their personal stories.

I have learned to see that situations in their lives, either past or current, are the reasons for the stress and ultimately the disorganization in their lives. I am writing this book to give you hope that your mess, your clutter, your disorganization is not too big to overcome, and neither is the story that goes with it.

Our stories, our struggles, and our messes; those are our common ground.

I was having dinner with a handful of influential women in the business community, each successful in her own right. I gazed around the table in awe, feeling grateful to have been invited to such a gathering. The women laughed and chatted and began to sing each other's praises, talking about successes the others had. Someone said to me, "Look at you, Lisa. You're making it happen. You've been on TV several times and have written a book. You get paid speaking engagements and have a growing business. That has to make you feel good." Funny though, I didn't see myself as their equal.

As the conversation progressed, one by one we opened up about our lives and the challenges we faced. For many of us we faced challenges with the kids, keeping up appearances and just the stress of day-to-day life. But as we continued to talk, some opened up about deeper things; their insecurities of not measuring up, the constant stress of chasing the next sale, the sadness and anger over a husband's infidelity and even physical abuse. Our struggles were as varied as our lives, yet we took comfort in knowing that we shared so many of the same common struggles.

I remember sitting there that night, stunned to learn that I was not alone in my struggles. There were women sitting all around me whom just minutes before had been laughing, all the while silently suffering because they feared they would be judged or their struggles misunderstood. What a relief to be able to take off our superwoman masks, let down our guards, and find such common ground.

On the outside chance that you, too, are wearing a mask, unable to let down your guard for fear someone might see behind your closed doors, I want to assure you, you are normal.

Whether you are a stay-at-home mom, a corporate executive, a teacher, a nurse, and a politician or any number of other roles, regardless, we all face the same daily battles and experiences. I have worked with hundreds of organizing clients and while no two situations are the same, much of what I have learned in life, I have learned from the wonderful people I have been able to help along the way. To protect the trust that my clients instill in me, I have changed names and details, but the stories in this book are absolutely real. It is my hope that in sharing their stories and my own personal journey, you may discover strength and purpose in the chaos of your life.

Chapter One
WHAT YOU HOLD ONTO

I often say that people are an accumulation of their experiences, and the things they accumulate tell of those experiences.

I had a bra once that I bought on the down-low when I was a teenager. I loved that bra, but in my household, it was absolutely considered contraband. It was black and lacy and everything my mother would have hated in a bra, which is in truth probably what I loved about it. I never wore that bra when I lived at home, mostly for fear someone would walk in on me in the bathroom or my bedroom and rat me out to our parents. But when I left home, I packed up my scandalous, black, lacy bra and moved it with me to take with me into my new married life.

Unfortunately, I hid the bra too well, and the box it ended up in the attic of our home. I did not discover the bra until many, many years later when moving from our home in Louisiana to our home in Texas. When I found it, I smiled, remembering the day I rebelliously purchased it and the feeling of strength and confidence that came with it.

Of course you know I could not resist trying it on!

Unfortunately, it didn't fit 'quite' the same way it fit when I was a teenager. Undeterred, I walked into our master bathroom to check myself out in the mirror. I can honestly say, I have not laughed that hard in a whole lot of years. I had parts squished together and spilling out in all kinds of places.

At one point, I turned to look at the back of the bra, causing the very old and very stretched fabric to tear loose from the single hook holding it all together. In one quick pop, my "girls" were set free, and I stood half-naked and laughing in hysteria. Oh my goodness, what a memory.

To this day, I still chuckle when I recall the surprise on my face when that bra popped open.

Why in the world am I telling you this story? Though I never wore that bra one single time as a teenager, I held onto it because it made me feel strong and beautiful and capable, things I didn't believe about myself as a teenage girl.

That's what we do. We hold onto things because they remind us of something we have experienced, something we have felt or believed, both for positive and negative reasons. And over time, those things we hold onto, whether tangible items or emotional baggage; they cause us to begin to unravel until eventually we become lost in a terrible cluttered mess of our own making.

Teresa's Story: A Ministry of Mess

The day I first arrived at Teresa's home she greeted me at the door with a frazzled smile and an entourage of small children. She and her husband, Kevin, apologetically moved laundry off the sofa and offered me a place to sit, both clearly embarrassed about the mess. "We travel a lot and so the laundry piles up," she said. "At the end of a long day, we just want to come home and relax and enjoy time with our kids. The last thing we want to do is cleaning and laundry." The children ran around and giggled and played. It was obviously a home of love.

Teresa and Kevin were ministers of a large church. They lived in a small home with three children and thought the answer to their clutter problem was to buy a larger home.

Teresa said to me, "Kevin and I realized that space is not our problem. We are just disorganized. We need to get this house in order and learn organizing strategies before we can buy a bigger home." She went on to say, "What kind of example am I providing for my children? And how am I supposed to minister to and help other women with messes in their personal lives when I can't help myself?" A valid question and one I had asked myself not so many years before.

Our first order of business was tackling their children's clothes. They had volumes. Volumes and volumes. She explained that many people gave them those clothes, and she felt she needed to save them for the younger children. The challenge was that they were continually receiving and buying more clothes. I said to Teresa, "You have more clothes than space, so you have two choices: more storage or purge." (That's pretty much always the choice!) Teresa replied, "I know we have too much. Kevin and I have already made peace with the fact that we need to get rid of some of these clothes." "Okay then," I said. "Pretend that none of these clothes belong to you and you need to buy them. They are all beautiful and you can see how useful they are. Now pretend that storage space is your money; what can you afford to buy?"

After a good bit of discussion, she agreed that she would release some of the clothes to the women's shelter. I gave her a black trash bag and said, "Whatever you are not keeping, we are going to put in this bag."

All of a sudden, she burst into tears and proceeded to tell me her story.

"When I was eight years old, my dad used to beat my mom. One night, my mom gave me a black trash bag and said, 'We are leaving. Whatever you can fit in this bag, we are taking and the rest has to stay.' Seeing that black trash bag made me remember that night." Teresa asked, "Do you think that is why I have been collecting so many things? Because I never wanted my children to feel they had a lack in their lives?"

Once we talked through that memory, and she made peace with it, it became easier for Teresa to release her "things" and continue the organizing process.

In twenty plus years of professional organizing I have seen "aha moments" more times than I can count. It's the "aha," the action that triggers the memory that triggers the understanding; THAT is the moment I wait for. I know it's coming, and when it does, I feel a great sense of relief for them because I know the freedom it will bring.

Their "aha" moment will be their first step in uncluttering their lives and their first step toward finding strength and purpose.

Chapter Two
WE'RE JUST ITALIANS

I am not a collector of things or a maker of messes. In fact, I am quite the opposite. I am a tidier, a straightener of things, a streamliner of processes. But nonetheless, my own life has been cluttered at times. Maybe not cluttered with too many things, as is the problem with many of my clients, but certainly cluttered with memories that affected how I lived out my life. Not so long ago, my cluttered memories, accumulated over time, spilled over from my mental world into my physical one. But I'm getting ahead of myself. Let me begin at the beginning.

I come from a long line of Italians, with a rich history, steeped in family and tradition and all that comes with it; the good, the bad, the loud, and the ugly. Grandma and Grandpa Buccola, my great-grandparents on my mom's side of the family, came to the United States from Palermo, Sicily, around 1920. Each widowed before their marriage to each other, Grandma came to the marriage with two children and Grandpa with five. Together they went on to have five more children, twelve children in all. The first nine children were born in Sicily, and the last three were born in the United States, a fact that my Mamaw Francis took great pride in. She liked to say, "I'm not an Italian; I'm an American."

Grandma and Grandpa Buccola owned two houses on General Haig Street in Lakeview, a suburb of New Orleans, Louisiana. Located across the street from one another, one was a double shotgun and the other was a little double house with one bedroom on each side. Over the years, various family members lived in one side of the shotgun or in the little double across the street. And many of the aunts and uncles lived nearby.

When Mamaw Francis was 13 years old, her daddy sold her to a 71-year-old man. By 16, she was old enough for him to marry her. And by 18, she divorced him and married my grandfather,

Philip Crosby. My mom, Judy, was the oldest of their three children. When my mom was only 13 years old, Mamaw Francis became very ill and had surgery. Mom was forced to care for her seven-year-old sister and one-year-old baby brother, a fact that made her grow up quickly, most said.

Mom was only 16 years old when she married my dad, who was only 18 years old himself. Neither one had graduated from high school. Dad earned a living as a paperboy. They said I was their love child, though back then it was viewed as a shame to the family. When I was first born, mom and dad lived in half of the little double across the street. Papaw got my daddy a job driving a truck for a cold cuts company. Mamaw Francis gave them some pots, dishes, a set of sheets, and some towels when they got married and said "You made your bed, now you're going to lie in it." Momma and Daddy were married for 31 years, until her death.

I was 14 months old, when my sister, Judy, was born. She was sickly with asthma and was hospitalized many times. I was sent to live with Mamaw Francis at first, because my mom couldn't care for a toddler and a sickly newborn. Eventually, my care was given to my aunt, who was 13 years old at the time. Mamaw Francis was just not up to taking care of a toddler, so I was passed around and cared for by the aunts and cousins. One of the cousins who cared for me was Arty, a teenager, who was later sent to Vietnam where he was killed in action. Trust me when I tell you, I was no stranger to loss.

Though being surrounded by loud, boisterous Italians as a small child was a blessing, I have often wondered how not having my mother around affected me. I can't say I remember how it felt to be bounced around from one place to another, too young to really comprehend what was going on, constantly losing those I loved, but I am sure the impact of her absence carried some weight in our relationship later on.

I recall that at one point, Mamaw Francis lived in half of the shotgun house. It was the most beautiful of places. In the mornings, as the sun came in the sidelights of the front door, you could hear the sound of doves cooing by the window. Just beyond the boundaries of that front door, was the fragrance of the ligustrum bushes and the sweet olive trees. And Mamaw's two dogs, Fawn and Pierre, one a German Sheppard and one a Dachshund, were always there to greet me with barks and tails wagging. We loved to torment those dogs by calling out to them and watching them run back and forth across the length of the fence, practically begging us to let them out. But we knew those silly dogs would escape if we let them out, so we never did.

Grandma and Grandpa Buccola had a huge front porch, and I enjoyed spending the weekends and summers there with my siblings and cousins. (Funny thing is, later in life when I went to see the house as an adult, the porch was quite small! To me, as a small child though, it was huge.) That porch was the gathering place for the family to drink coffee and talk. New Orleans was hot and humid, with only a couple of months in the year that were cool. Many families in that area during the 1960's did not have a central air conditioner, so the porch provided a breeze from the summer heat. The kids would swing on the black iron railings of the porch and drop off into the bushes below. Sometimes we got stung by the wasps in the bushes, but it never deterred us. To this day, I love homes with a porch.

Grandma and the aunts were usually in the kitchen cooking and visiting with one another. When they weren't cooking, they were playing pokeno or canasta card games. The uncles were business owners and realtors, and though they didn't separate from the women socially, they were actively engaged in their own loud conversations.

Grandpa Buccola was a very stern man who spoke no English. He spent most of his time sitting on the end of the sofa eating spaghetti from a metal TV tray and watching the television. We kids liked to stand at the end of the sofa and stare at him, almost daring him to catch us. But boy if he caught us staring, he'd snarl at us, and we'd run off either giggling or fearing for our lives.

One thing about that house and family growing up, there was always lots of laughter and loud voices. I loved being a part of that loud and rowdy family. It gave me a true sense of where I came from and where I belong. I still love being surrounded by large groups of people.

Cherie's Story – On Fire

Cherie was the owner of two businesses. She knew her house was a mess, but blamed it on her busy schedule, four children, and a messy husband. After all, it was very stressful to manage so many employees, all the overhead, and the pressure of keeping new jobs rolling in.

When I met Cherie, she was planning a big anniversary party for her parents at her home, and she wanted to get things in order. The first day we worked together she answered the door dressed in jeans and a t-shirt with her hair pulled back. Her demeanor was very forthright and direct. As we started, I proceeded to ask her my usual assessment questions. Her response was "This is hard enough. I don't want to talk about anything; let's just do this."

"Alrighty then," I thought in my head. "It's gonna be that kind of job."

As we began the organizing process, I engaged her in humor to lighten the mood. The weight of her serious demeanor required me to be more light-hearted than usual (which is saying quite a bit, considering my loud Italian ways). Later in the day as we were leaving to go and pick up containers, I told her son, "If we are not back in a couple of hours, one of us killed the other one." She laughed, and we walked out the door like two old friends.

As we rode to the store, I told Cherie one of my client's stories (as I often do in an anonymous way). Cherie said to me, "When I was a little girl, one day at school we heard the fire engines going down the road, I thought, 'Wow someone's house is burning.' When I got home from school, I realized it was my home. I ran inside to find that I had lost all my toys and things." Then she said, "I don't know why I remembered that. Maybe that's why I like to collect things." She laughed light-heartedly but I could tell she had just made an important discovery about herself and her clutter.

Cherie had already made peace with beginning the decluttering and organizing, her memory of losing her toys in the fire only served as a reflection and reminder as she continued the process of uncluttering her life.

13

Chapter Three
CLOSE, CRAMPED AND CLUTTERED

Mom and Dad moved away from Lakeview to Avondale when I was still a toddler. Avondale is on the other side of the Mississippi River from Lakeview, the West bank of the New Orleans metropolitan area. It was hard on my mom to be so far away from her mom, dad, and family. But for my dad, whose parents had divorced when he was a toddler, it didn't seem to matter as much. He didn't really have a close relationship with his family and they were more spread out across the city.

Dad moved us to Avondale because he wanted to live close to the shipyard where he worked. I grew up in a lower middle class neighborhood, though my cousin, told me I should say, "A poor neighborhood." But I didn't view myself as poor. Daddy said that we had more than he had growing up. He lived in the projects and only ate meat once a week. He said the rule in his house growing up was "whoever eats the fastest eats the most." He said "We have food, clothes, and a roof over our head; and that's all anyone needs."

Thankfully, my mom was a great cook and seamstress, though I hated wearing homemade clothes. Some of the kids in school use to tease me about my homemade clothes, which of course made matters worse. It wasn't my mama's sewing that bothered me (most days), but I just wanted to be like the other kids and wear store bought clothes. I felt like even among the other poor kids that I didn't belong.

I remember one time my mom made me this horrible outfit that made me look like a giant baby wearing it. It had polka dots all over it and a huge button in the back. The morning she made me wear it to school, I just about died. But I quickly came up with a plan. The minute I got to school, I went into the Principal's office and told him I was sick. When my mama got there to pick me up, she didn't say, "How do you feel?" She said,

"You really hate that outfit, don't you?" She was mad, but it was so worth it to me. I didn't win many battles, but I sure won that one.

Our 900 square foot home was a tight squeeze for our family of six and often housed family and friends who were down on their luck. There was always room on our couches and floors when someone was in need. To make matters worse, we had one bathroom. So, if one person was taking a bath and someone had to use the bathroom, it was the honor system to keep the door unlocked and the shower curtain closed. Of all my childhood memories, this one still sends me over the edge! It was just creepy to think that on the other side of my bath curtain MIGHT be a grown man, friend, or family, doing his business, so to speak. And heaven forbid they had to do number two! I will say this; I did learn how to hold my breath for a really long time underwater!

Still, like my daddy said, we had all we needed. We always had clothes and food and a place to sleep. But while we might have had all we needed, my childhood home was a disaster with a capital D. I guess you could say that my mom may have been chronically disorganized. I don't think we were collectors; there was no money for that. But what we lacked in money, we made up for in messiness.

For example, like most homes, space was at a premium in our house, especially storage space. So, my mom's clothes closet was the front closet, just inside the entryway of our home. One of the most embarrassing things to me growing up what that my mom always hung her bra on the doorknob to that front entryway closet. Her BRA. You know how some people kick their shoes off the second they come into a house? Well I guess with my mama it was her bra, because I couldn't think of a single other reason that bra had to hang on that doorknob. She must have burst through the door with one hand behind her back, unhooking that thing, yanking it off and hanging it on the first thing handy, namely, the doorknob. It's funny now, but back then it was a big source of embarrassment.

Another source of embarrassment for me was our kitchen. The kitchen counter had two hideous harvest gold, round turntables; one for spices and one for medicine. Just let your mind's eye get a picture of that for a second. And if that wasn't bad enough, our kitchen table was covered with stuff. I longed for a table with a pretty centerpiece. The shows on TV had fruit bowls or flower arrangements on the center. But mine had boxes of cereal, baggies, socks, toys, random batteries that no one knew if they still worked, and LOTS of mail.

I guess you could say I was never really "at home" in my home growing up. It wasn't the fact that our home was small that made me feel that way, but that it was messy and not pretty. I couldn't understand why my friends' houses were pretty and mine was not. I tried hard to organize our home and 'fix it up' and put stuff away, but I always had resistance from my family. If they couldn't find something, it was my fault. They called me the white tornado, and not in a loving way.

Since I couldn't organize my home, I decorated and organized my bedroom and the top of my dresser. But when my sister, Judy, polished furniture and vacuumed, she always moved my things and didn't put them back. It was very upsetting to me because all I wanted was my own pretty space. To this day, if you move my stuff on my counters or tables I may get upset. My husband moved my canisters on the kitchen counter the other day and didn't put it back, and I freaked out. I just want people to leave my stuff alone. (Irony that I now move people's stuff as my business; but I do have their permission to do so.)

Joan's Story – They Are Just Children

Joan was a nurse and floor supervisor for a large hospital system. When she decided to move to a new city to be closer to her family, Joan called a realtor to put her home on the market. The realtor was appalled at the condition of her home and told her to clean it up first. So Joan called me in to guide the process of getting her home ready for a sale.

The first day that I arrived, Joan was so relieved that someone was there to help her. Up unto my arrival, the moving process felt like such a monumental task for one person to handle. She had no support from her husband who had challenges with collecting broken things to fix. Cleaning house was not her priority. Joan's priority was most assuredly her children. She beamed as she showed me the paper plate with gold spray painted macaroni and yarn that her daughter created.

Because her children were small, Joan was preoccupied with creating a happy and fun environment for her children; so preoccupied that she neglected her household. I suggested that she engage her eight and ten-year-old in the organizing process. She snapped back, "They are just children."

(I have learned that when I strike a nerve, my clients usually strike back, and I had clearly struck a nerve.)

When I sensed her anxiety, I asked her why she felt they were too young to help in the organizing process. She snapped, "My sister and I were forced to clean the house on Saturdays and there was never enough time to watch TV or play. I don't want that for my children." As gently as I could, I replied, "Joan, just like everything in life, there needs to be balance. Just like we teach our children to read, write and brush their teeth, we do them a disservice by not teaching them to help around the house." I proceeded to share how I taught my children to do chores at ages six and eight. I set up a chore chart for my children with the reward of allowance at the end of the week. I suggested that the children only be given allowance when they had earned it by completing a task. I explained that as my children got older, I gave them a limited budget for clothing and shoes, and earning money allowed them to buy the name brands they wanted. My children enjoyed being able to buy things for themselves.

Once she saw how she could practically accomplish getting her kids involved without feeling she was denying her children fun, Joan began to engage her children in the organizing process. No longer was the job just left to her, but it became family responsibility (as it should be).

Sometimes in the process of uncluttering, we discover things hidden in the recesses, unexplored until we are forced to let a little light in. Helping Joan realize that her childhood memories were causing the clutter in her life gave her the strength to make necessary changes. By addressing her own anxiety and feelings from her past, she established new habits for her children and her home and kicked her clutter goodbye.

Chapter Four
GROWING UP YEARS

There are parts of my childhood that were so normal, so typical of the times that we could have been a poster family for the decade. Our family looked like the ideal working class family. Dad worked a blue-collar job, and Mom stayed at home with the kids. Overall, we were fairly well adjusted, despite our move away from family out to Avondale. I settled right in to our new life there, quickly making friends, as was my nature.

I loved having a large group of friends, all kids from the "popular crowd," which was a bonus for a girl who struggled a good bit with her self-image. I was a short, dark-haired, Italian girl with a dark complexion and a love for food. (A fact that my daddy was more than happy to remind me of on a regular basis). I stood in stark contrast to my tall, blonde, fair-skinned friends, and sometimes I let the comparison get to me. Let's just say that having friends from the in-group was a wonderful boost to my self-image.

We all lived in the same neighborhood because back then very few people in our socio-economic class moved around. We were in classes together from second grade all the way through high school. We were such good friends that I still remember their names to this day.

As kids, we rode bikes together, played games, had sleepovers, explored the woods behind the neighborhood, and ran through the sprinklers. In the mornings, as we walked to the bus stop, many of our moms stood outside in the street with curlers in their hair, bathrobes on, cigarette in one hand and a cup of coffee in the other hand. They weren't standing there to keep watch over us like moms do today; they were out there because it was the time of day mom's socialized. I always imagined them standing there long after the bus had collected us all, chatting about things like husbands and recipes until their cigarettes burned up or their coffee cups were emptied.

As I grew older, I played the flute and eventually joined the marching band at school. It was so great to get to march at our football games and in Mardi Gras parades. The band was my community, my people as they say today. We had some great times at those Mardi Gras parades too, and learned a whole lot about human anatomy! (If you have ever been to a Mardi Gras parade, you know what I'm talking about! They are definitely not G rated!)

By high school, we were planning our futures, whom we would marry (in our dreams) and what colleges we would attend. Since neither of my parents had graduated from high school, they weren't very supportive of my desire to go to college. My mentor at the time said "Lisa, if you think you ever want to stay home with children; don't waste your parents' money with college." I valued her advice, and I knew I wouldn't win the battle with my parents anyway, so I put my dream of going to college away.

I felt so isolated from my school friends. As they planned their future lives and talked excitedly about where they would go to college, I tried to make peace with my new future. But peace would be a long time coming for me.

Jenna's Story – Someone Else's Version Of You

Jenna was a successful realtor in the community. Part of her marketing strategy was the involvement in her local country club. She enjoyed playing golf and tennis with the affluent ladies in the community. She liked to call them "the princesses," which was funny because her husband laughed and told me, "She's a princess herself."

Image was everything to Jenna.

Jenna had a smile on at all times, and one would think she was happy and content. But inside, Jenna lived with a constant internal need for everyone to like her and do business with her. It has been my experience with my clients that anytime we work overly hard at putting a polished look on our inner turmoil, it bubbles up somewhere in the form of a cluttered mess. Jenna's mess was in her office, a paperwork disaster, and three computers, two that didn't work. Jenna's only thought was the next sale.

As I sat with her and we talked like I do with all my clients, she shared a story that gave me some insight into her driven personality. She said to me, "The other day I was having lunch with my girlfriends and one of my friends announced her house was on the market, and all I could think was, 'Why didn't she use me as a realtor?'"

As she told her story, her voice trailed off and she said, "Why am I so consumed with success?" Though I didn't have an answer for her, I'd venture to guess her desire to be successful and well thought of came from someplace deep in her past.

I replied, "Jenna, I don't have an answer for you, but at the end of the day, you have to decide what you want in life. Otherwise, you'll spend the rest of your life trying to be someone else's version of you."

Finding our strength and our purpose requires us to understand and accept ourselves; the real version of us, not the version we try so hard to become.

Chapter Five
DARK DAYS

As my friends excitedly went about planning their lives, I developed clinical depression and an anxiety disorder. But people around me did not understand depression. They said, "What do you have to be depressed about?" They also said I needed to "snap out of it" or that I must have some secret sin I was hiding. I knew as much about depression as my friends and family did so I thought to myself that they might be right. Desperate to feel better, one night I sat down with my dad and confessed everything I had ever done that might have been remotely wrong. As I sat before him, baring my soul of every real or perceived indiscretion, my dad sat before me like a robot. No sign of emotion crossed his face. There was no notable movement in his posture. He just sat there. When I finally finished speaking, I expected him to reach out, put his arm around me, and tell me I was going to be okay. But his only response was, "If you've been hiding all this, what else are you hiding?" Whoever said confession is good for the soul didn't know my dad.

My dad's rejection of me in that moment made me feel like everything I did was wrong. From that moment forward, I constantly second-guessed myself and searched for answers. I read all the self-help books on positive thinking and overcoming depression that I could put my hands on, but in the end those only left me anxious and more confused.

I was so plagued by guilt and feelings of inadequacy that I felt if I just did my very best and lived a perfect life, I wouldn't be depressed or struggle with anxiety anymore. I wish someone would have asked me, "How's that working for you?" In short, it didn't work. It only served to help me create a life bound up in legalism and rules. The more I perceived myself to be "good" the worse everyone and everything around me became, until eventually I developed a very self-righteous attitude that plagued me almost all of my adult life.

As a high school student striving to be perfect, I sank deeper and deeper into my depression. Staying in school proved to be a tremendous struggle as well. Because I had my own car and drove myself to school, when things got tough, I just left. Can you imagine my parents at this point? On the one hand there was this girl living in their home trying to abide by every rule, even ones she'd created on her own. And on the other hand, they had this teenager skipping school whenever she felt like it. I was a chaotic mess. Eventually, my parents took my car away, and I was forced to ride the bus, which was terribly humiliating. As my friends seemed to have a bright future ahead of them, I seemed to be regressing, rapidly.

I somehow made it through the holidays and the spring, but six short weeks before graduation, I was having such difficulty coping that I went to my guidance counselor and said, "I am quitting school." She was very kind and concerned and would NOT let me drop out. Had it not been for her, I most likely would not have finished. But I did finish, and I managed to graduate with all A's and one B; but trust me when I tell you, it was a miracle I graduated at all.

The October after I graduated from high school, I felt like I was having a nervous breakdown. Momma finally decided to take me to the doctor, and when the doctor found out that I had been in this state for over seven months, he had me committed to the psychiatric unit of the hospital for 32 days. It sounds weird to say, but I actually enjoyed being there. The psych techs talked to me and didn't judge me. I spent my days making crafts and feeling normal for the first time in a long time. There was no one to please and no one to disappoint. I wasn't thinking about my future or my friends or my family. I was at peace.

The medicine they gave me numbed all the thoughts that swirled in my mind and were a welcome relief to the mental anguish I'd been in for so long. Finally, after a month in their care, I was discharged. Momma and I rode in silence in the car for a good long while. I could see the struggle of her thoughts by the way she continually creased the space between her eyebrows. She'd open her mouth as if she had something to say, and then close it without so much as a word. Eventually my gaze turned from my momma's face as I leaned my face up against the window of the car. I rode the rest of the way home in silence, looking out the window and noticing for the first time that fall had overtaken my New Orleans home.

As we pulled into the driveway, Momma looked over at me and finally spoke. She said, "The medicine you are on makes you a zombie. You look stupid, Lisa." I had come so far in learning to realize that depression wasn't my "fault" so her words were hurtful. But looking back, I don't blame my parents. They had no idea what to do with me. It was 1980, and there was such a stigma and ignorance attached to mental disorders. Plain and simple, I was an embarrassment to my family.

Kay's Story – A Safe Place

I arrived at Kay's home and was greeted by a very loud and friendly voice. She made me feel like family right away with her delightful and welcoming personality. Kay was an artist and her home looked like an art museum. Artwork and signs of her creativity could be seen throughout her home. She delighted in giving me the tour of her home and everything had a fun story to go with it. What a delight.

Kay called me to organize her studio and her children's playroom. The studio was a large task, but it was relatively easy to put in order and set up new systems. We brought in shelving, sorted, and grouped like items. Nothing was discarded because according to Kay, everything is useful to an artist. I didn't really think too much about her seeming unwillingness to part with things because, well, I'm not an artist, and I thought her logic made sense. I thought it made sense until we got to the playroom.

The playroom was another story. There was not a place to move with all of the toys. Many of the toys her children had either outgrown or were no longer interested in playing with. She became upset at the very mention of getting rid of some of the toys. She was adamant in the fact that we needed to figure out how to organize around them. As I continued my assessment with her, I discovered that she lost both of her parents as a little girl. She was raised by an aunt on a fixed income. Not only did she feel abandoned by not having parents, she felt deprived of toys. She wanted to give everything she didn't have to her children.

Once I understood Kay's needs, we were able to come up with a doable plan. We decked her attic and created functional space for the unused toys. This allowed her to feel she still had them. The attic was a safe place to store her things and her memories until she was ready to let them all go.

There are times when my clients realize why they are doing the things they do, and they are willing to make a change right away. But there are times in the process of uncluttering they need more time to process. For some the change may come a year later and for others, they may never want the change.

The truth of the matter is, we can store away the things we don't want to deal with, and for a short time, that might be the best solution. But if we truly want to find strength and purpose in the midst of chaos, at some point, we have to unclutter. Eventually, like it or not, the contents of our lives spill over and we are faced with no other choice but to face our mess.

Chapter Six

THE LAND IN BETWEEN

ollowing graduation, I lived at home for years. The land in between childhood and adulthood is a weird place, especially when you are an adult living at home. Though I felt God had healed me from my depression, I still struggled with feelings of guilt and inadequacy, in part, I think due to my dad's very dominant personality.

Dad and I had a difficult relationship. I always felt he loved me, but I never felt cherished by him. It seemed to be an internal struggle of his, one I wouldn't understand for many years to come. He was my dad. He loved me, and he took care of me. He was a strong disciplinarian at times, and other times he cooed on me as his beautiful princess. There were moments I longed for dad's affection and other times I feared his harshness.

Dad was very legalistic as well. I was taught never to question authority, especially that of my parents, and that continued even into my adulthood. If I had an opinion different from theirs and spoke it, I was criticized, condemned, and corrected. I didn't realize I could respect authority and have a difference of opinion until I was a much older woman. I was told the two cancelled each other out. If I did something contrary to their direction, I was told I was rebellious and unteachable. I was constantly criticized and told my dreams and comments were a "little out there.'"

One morning, my momma and I were getting into it over something seemingly insignificant. I was 21 years olds, well old enough to make all decisions for myself (at least legally) but because I was still living under their roof, I was expected to follow their orders much like I had done as a child. As I said, living at home as an adult but still feeling very much like a child is a strange place to be. As Momma and I continued our discussion, Daddy sat at the table reading his paper, I guess pretending he didn't hear Momma's rant, but Lord knows the neighbors could hear her by that point.

Momma stood at the kitchen sink washing dishes from our breakfast and continued her rant about how stupid I could be sometimes. I finally had enough and told her I was grown woman and could do what I wanted whether she liked it or not.

You can imagine how that went over. Momma put the dish down she was washing, dried her hands calmly on her apron, walked slowly to where I was sitting at the kitchen table and slapped me straight across the face. I sat in stunned silence, tears stinging my eyes and the heat of her hand stinging my face as the whelps slowly appeared on my cheeks. I looked at Daddy for support of some kind (because clearly my momma had just crossed the line) but he looked at me over the top of his paper and shrugged his shoulders as if to say, "Well Lisa, what did you expect was going to happen?"

That was the culture of my family and I took the correction as my fault. But deep inside, I was angry with her for striking me and angry with him for not protecting me. And more than that, I was angry for not being allowed to be a grown up with a mind of her own. Why could I not have my own opinion? Why was everything I wanted viewed as wrong? Once I got past the anger, then I felt guilt. It somehow always returned to guilt and shame, a cycle I lived with until a catastrophic event in my life forced me to make a lasting change.

Cathy's Story – Only the Lonely

I ran into an old friend that I hadn't seen in a long time the other day. We were both surprised to see each other. We went to school together in New Orleans, and both of us were a long way from home.

Cathy invited me to lunch. She had such a pretty smile, but there was sadness in her voice. "How are you?" I asked. After the basic niceties of what brought her and her husband to this town, she began to cry. "I hate living here. I'm so lonely. Moving here was supposed to keep him from traveling, but he works 15 hour days, it's like his job is more important than me." I gave her hug and said, "I understand. Have you considered getting a part time job or a volunteer project to help you not feel so lonely"? "That's the problem," she said quietly with her head down. "Tom said I didn't need to work and to just relax, but I was bored and wanted someone to talk to." Cathy continued. "I'm so embarrassed. I have a big problem." I had a feeling I knew what she was going to say next. "Promise you won't tell anyone," Cathy said. "I promise," I replied. "I am seeing someone else," she said, "I never meant for it to happen. He was one of the committee members from a fundraiser I worked on. I don't know what to do. He makes me feel so special. He talks to me. He understands me. I think I love him."

At this point, she was sobbing hard. "I don't have anyone else I can talk to, Lisa," Cathy said. "And ever since I started with this relationship - you should see my house. I'm stressed. I can't sleep and my stomach always hurts." She went on, almost like once the switch had clicked on, she couldn't stop. "I had no one to talk to which only made it worse for me and Tom. I feel like all Tom does is criticize and speak rudely to me. I don't deserve to be treated this way. It would be so nice if Tom would give me attention and talk nice to me like this other man."

It's in times like these that I know what the logical and moral answer is, but for me it was to speak the truth in love and support her. In time, she went for counseling. I can't say what she decided. For every person it's different. Verbal abuse, loneliness, & lack of romance and communication are difficult subjects. Some women choose to work it out and stay married, especially if the spouse is willing to seek counseling as well. For other women, they feel that they're finished with the marriage, especially if too many years have gone and the love has become cold.

Cathy's life had become a cluttered mess, and reaching out to talk to someone was her first step in becoming uncluttered. Before you get caught in the infidelity trap or even if you already are, get support from a trusted friend or counselor. You can't keep it in.

Chapter Seven
A FAIRY TALE MARRIAGE

I met Joseph Giesler at church, a blue-collar worker like my dad and a man who shared my faith. At the time, I was driving around in a new car with a color called "bittersweet." Joe teased me all time saying, "When are you going to take me for a ride in that orange glow car of yours?" I loved his good-natured teasing and finally said, "If you buy me a ticket to the concert next week, I'll drive you." Our first date was to the concert with my sister and my mom in the back seat, but funny thing is, I didn't actually realize it was our first date until our third date. (That might seem like a funny statement, but at the time, I had a string of boys I was "seeing" and so Joe just kind of blended into the scenery.)

But by our third date, Joe most definitely stood out from the crowd. Joe proposed to me on our third date, which looking back seems crazy to me, but that's how Joe works. Once his mind is made up, he doesn't waste time. At first, I said yes, but a few days later, I got cold feet and said I wanted to take the time to think and pray. Joe didn't put any pressure on me. Everything inside of me felt like he was the right one, but I wanted to be sure. In October, just two months after our first date, I accepted his proposal.

I remember the first time Joe was introduced to my extended Italian family. The kitchen was crowded and since I was the smallest, I had to sit in the back corner of the table. Joe was sitting on the outside of the table by the counter since he was the tallest. Mamaw said, "Lisa, Joe is out of root beer. Get him some more." I said, "Mamaw, he is right there. He can reach it himself, and I am all the way in this corner." But that's not the way a Buccola woman treated her man. Mamaw quickly set me straight and said, "No Lisa, you take care of that man." So, I squirmed out of my seat and got up and fixed Joe more root beer. A little bit later Mamaw said, "Lisa, Joe is out of bread. Get him some more." But it had been such a hassle getting up to get his drink, this time I insisted, "Mamaw, he is right there. He can reach it easier than I can." But once again, she insisted, "No Lisa, you take care of that man," she replied again. At that point, it was no use arguing, and I knew it. Funny thing is that years later Joe admitted that he knew right then and there that he was going to enjoy my family. His mom didn't serve his dad, but he definitely liked being served.

Six months after our first date, Joe and I were married. We had a small intimate wedding, certainly not the wedding of my dreams, but I didn't really have a say in the matter according to Momma. The only thing that mattered at the time was that I was married and finally out on my own. I was so unprepared for the reality of marriage though. I guess I thought when I was married I'd finally have my own space. Imagine my shock when I realized I now had to share with Joe! I think that reality set in when we had been married for two weeks, and Joe came in the bathroom, sat on the toilet seat, opened up the shower curtain and said, "Hi!" I was very angry and said, "Excuse me! Do you mind? I am taking a bath! Can I have my privacy?!" Joe was quite taken aback. He replied, "Lisa, we are married! What is the deal?" He was right. I guess because growing up the bath was my only type of privacy, I was just shocked that he picked THAT moment to have a conversation.

Avondale was the neighborhood that I was raised in. Highway 90 divided the subdivision. I was raised on the north side by the railroad, and Joe and I bought a home on the south side of highway 90. We didn't have a lot of money, but it was important to me for my house to look nice. My married friends and I often looked through decorating magazines and then went to yard sales on Friday looking for items to decorate our homes. (You had to go the yard sale on the first day to get the best stuff.) I wanted my home to be pretty, to be a place to entertain company, and not be embarrassed. There would be no lazy-susans on MY kitchen table, no cluttered messes in my living room, and for darn sure there would not be a bra hanging on my entryway door!

I enjoyed the freedom in taking care of my own home, organizing and decorating it to my heart's content. It gave me a sense of pride and control. And for once in my life, I actually enjoyed having company over. I also enjoyed the familiarity of living in the neighborhood I grew up in, even if we did live on the other side of the highway. I loved knowing everyone at the gas station, grocery store, drug store, the five-and-dime store, and the auto parts store. The downside to living in such a small town is that everyone knows everyone else's business, including Momma and Daddy. Whenever I bought something at a yard sale or did something in the community, Momma had something negative to say about it. I loved my mom and just wanted her to be proud of me. I thought taking care of my home and making it look nice would be a way we could connect. Heck, I'd have settled for just some nice adult dialog like, "Oh Lisa, I heard you got a coffee table. I'll have to come see it." Lord knows that's not how things went though.

The cycle was always the same. Momma would call and be negative about something I'd said or done. If I argued with her, Daddy would call and give me the guilt trip about my disrespect. (You don't know what a guilt trip is until you've grown up in an Italian Catholic family!) One day, Joe had enough. He stormed over to the princess trimline phone hanging on our kitchen wall and punched in the number like a man on a mission. With as much force in his voice as he'd displayed punching in the number, he told my dad on the other end of the line, "You take care of things on your side of the highway, and I will take care of things on my side of the highway."

Though I loved how Joe stood up to my daddy and declared that I was his, marriage to Joe was rough in the beginning. Joe had lived alone for ten years before we were married, so he didn't think he needed to be accountable to me. He had times when he left to take a ride and never even bothered to tell me. He also wasn't very romantic. We were married, but it sure wasn't like the fairy tale marriage I had envisioned as a girl.

Joe and I came from two different worlds growing up. He was my total opposite. They say that opposites attract, but opposites also attack. Joe said I was always trying to put him in a box to make him like my family. In some ways that was true. I was tied more to the beliefs of my parents than to my husband. I believed everything that my parents said, so if Joe wanted to do something contrary to their opinion or to my upbringing, whether spiritually, financially, celebrating holidays, or anything else, I thought we should do it my parent's way. Joe often had outbursts of anger. He never hit me, but he sure did yell and curse. He always apologized later, but he usually said it was my fault.

We never seemed to get past certain issues, but I tried to concentrate on the good of Joe and our marriage and not the negative. Joe grew up in a liberal household and was (and is) a very fun person. At times, he was full of mischief and often laughed at my naivety. One night as we were leaving the neighborhood I said, "Joe, look how bright the moon is over there!" He jerked the wheel of the car quickly and said, "Want to go that way and get a closer look?" "Can we?" I asked. It wasn't until he busted out laughing that I realized he was teasing me. Most of the time, I enjoyed Joe's good-natured teasing and laughter, even if it was at my expense. It was a great stress reliever for the stress of those early years of marriage.

Paulette's Story – Normal

I always wondered what it would be like to be a public figure or to be married to a public figure. I have had the opportunity to work with a few of them on an intimate basis. Paulette was a very confident and gracious woman. Her house was meticulous, but like many people, the paperwork had gotten out of hand. The volumes of paperwork and mail that came to her home caused her great stress. There were multiple categories of paperwork for her to deal with too. She had her husband's mail, her personal mail, the household bills, the children's schoolwork and artwork, and then she had all the additional community projects that come with being a public figure's wife.

As we began to work, she expressed that her bigger concern was for her children. Her desire was to create as normal of a life as possible. "When you are in the public eye as much as we are, people expect your home and children to be perfect. Our schedules are so crazy, I have yet to figure out how to balance this all. It's not just the paperwork, it's everything," she lamented.

I felt for Paulette. Her life was so much different than most of the people I knew and even many of the clients I knew. I said to her, "This is definitely something that other families don't encounter, but you are right in wanting to protect your children. It is important to provide as normal of a life as possible for them. They need to know that even though people are sometimes not nice, they can always count on you. Just keep the conversations open with them." I replied to her.

Working with Paulette and admiring her desire to have a normal life and a normal relationship with her children made me realize that I had been holding on to some things from my own childhood that I needed to work through. I think it was the first time I realized that working in other people's messes and helping them sort through their clutter was helping me unclutter my own world.

Chapter Eight
STAY AT HOME MOM

After four and a half years of marriage, we had our first son, Joseph (JoJo) and two years later, our second son, Charles (Charlie), was born. I wanted to have another child, but all my friends said, "If you have more than two, you won't be able to put them in private school." So once again, I listened to others, and believed my priority should be on saving for private school and not growing my family.

As a young, stay-at-home mom, I dreamed of owning my own business. I felt embarrassed when working women with college degrees asked me very piously (in my opinion) "What do you do?" Something about answering, "I'm a stay-at-home" was so embarrassing. I don't know why I was embarrassed; it was my choice to stay at home, and I certainly do not regret those years. Time as a stay-at-home mom was what mattered most to me back then. I still laugh when I think about the boys coming inside with their little faces covered in mud with just the whites of their eyes and teeth showing. Or the day I was baking homemade biscuits and the boys were outside playing with frogs. They ran into the house and before I could yell "Boys!" they were into the dough, offering "help" with my baking. But even with my obsessive-compulsive germ issues, I graciously baked the biscuits and ate them. Those are memories and years I will always treasure.

Still, I often felt like I was missing something. I thumbed through magazines in the checkout at the grocery store, trying to find my niche. When I was pregnant with Charlie, I even began writing a book on organization. I knew organizing was my gift and would someday be how I'd make a living. I approached family members and they just thought it was such an unattainable thing to be a published author. I even had a relative who owned a printing company, but he was going to charge me an enormous amount of money to print it; which I didn't have. I couldn't get anyone to see my dream and help me. I registered as a business, typed my first booklet, purchased a post office box, put an ad in a local paper, and sold one booklet. When my only customer inquired about my credentials, I became afraid that I would be exposed as a fraud. I had no one to guide me in starting or running a business. And Joe was always looking at the practical side and felt it would be a huge personal and financial distraction. I was such a dreamer, but I put that first little book away in a file box, which I still have.

Meredith's Story – A Cry For Help

A woman named Meredith called. "My boyfriend and his daughter are moving in with me, and I need to make room for his stuff," she said on our initial phone call. I arrived at the house and was greeted by Meredith in a suit and lab coat. She managed several clinics around the city. Her boyfriend, John, was retired from the police force, and it was obvious that he was used to being in control. He was a very large and intimidating man and when he spoke, his voice was loud and bellowing. "She needs to get rid of this ugly furniture" he said. "But that one and that one I like," she replied. My concern was how he talked down to her. "She is an educated woman who gains respect from so many employees and doctors," I thought.

On my second visit, John was not there and Meredith was wearing a tank top. The back of her arms and back were covered with bruises. "I need to make sure that all these clothes go the women's shelter when they are donated. You know sometimes women have to escape during the night, and they have clothes there for them," she said. I knew in that moment she was trying to say something to me. I took her outside so the children couldn't hear us talk. "I know what you are going through, Meredith." I said to her. "How can you tell?" she asked, obviously concerned. I said to her. "You don't have to live like this, Meredith. Making room for John in your life isn't why I'm here. It's to help you see you don't have to."

The most important thing for a woman in this type of situation is to get help. Call your local woman's shelter or find a trusted friend that will truly speak into your life and help you. After all those years of wondering what my niche in the world was, I realized it was to help people. Sometimes I am there to help them unclutter a room and sometimes I am there to help them unclutter their life.

Chapter Nine

FAMILY TRAGEDY: ANGER AND REGRET

The year after Joe and I were married, Mom was diagnosed with breast cancer. The doctor removed one breast and gave her two radiation treatments. They said she didn't need chemotherapy because the cancer was only in seven lymph nodes, and they thought they had all of it. Her insurance at the time was an HMO policy and they would not permit her to see an oncologist. It was up to her primary care physician to determine if she needed an oncologist. The year between the births of my two sons, mom was having trouble walking with pain in her hip. She was being treated with steroids for bursitis. My sister was working as a nurse at the time and confronted the doctor, demanding him to order a bone scan. The scan revealed that the cancer had spread throughout her bones.

The next few years were grueling. She endured two different types of chemotherapy alternating with two extensive radiation treatments. My mom required constant care, and there was tremendous pressure for me to care for her because I was the oldest. My sister lived in Oklahoma and my brother was away at college. Eventually my brother quit college and his job to care for mom while dad worked.

The truth of the matter was I *couldn't* take care of my mom. I had two small children who needed me and my relationship with my mom was beyond strained. If I'm honest with myself and with you, I didn't like my mom. I know that sounds harsh and probably wrong, but that was how I felt. I loved her as my mom. But she had been always critical of what I wanted to do or be and after so many years of trying, I had just shielded myself from her scrutiny and constant disapproval. Caring for her full-time felt like I was opening myself all over again.

Over the years, I tried to have a relationship with Mom, but every time I let her in, I got hurt. Once when I was pregnant with my oldest son, my mom's first grandchild, we went out to eat together. I remember thinking a grandbaby would be something we could bond over. As we were eating, enjoying our time together, one of mom's friends spotted us and came to the table to say a quick hello. I fully expected Mom to gush about her first grandbaby being on the way, but instead she bragged about everyone and everything else. When her friend enquired about her kids, my mom said, "Well, Judy is a nurse, Andy is in college, and Phil is in the Army." Then almost as an afterthought she said, "Oh and this is Lisa." Not one word about me having her first grand baby. Once again, I felt overlooked and unimportant in her world.

It was horrible watching her suffer. She couldn't walk and was in constant pain. On Monday, August 23, 1993, at 6:30 p.m., my mom died. I remember that day well. My Aunt and I had been at the house all day. We were going through mom's things, wanting to spare my dad as much as we could, and knowing her death was imminent. I remember as we were going in and out of the house taking things to the car, the screen door slammed and she jumped. I felt cruel for not closing the door quietly, but I was just so angry with her that I didn't really care. Just a few days earlier, mom had made a deathbed statement that shocked the family, telling us of an affair she'd had. After that, she was no longer able to speak. By her last day, she was unresponsive and unable to communicate in any way, so I knew that slamming screen door must have hurt her.

When I arrived home from Momma's that afternoon, Joe called to say he had tickets to the Saints game and thought it would be good for me to get away. When we arrived at the Superdome, I called from a payphone to check on the boys. The boys were at my next-door neighbor's house, and after I asked about them, I asked, almost in fear of what the answer might be, "Can you check and see if my dad has called?" Her cordless phone had reception in my house, so she was always gracious to check on things for me. She said, "Let me check and listen to the recorder." She held her phone up to my answering machine and pressed play. As soon as I heard my dad's voice on the phone, my heart froze. He said, "Mom's gone. Come home, Lisa." My emotions in that moment were all over the place. I was overcome with sadness and grief because my mom was dead. And I was filled with regret and guilt over a lifetime of struggling to love and be loved by her. And I was filled with relief, both that she was no longer in pain, and that we would no longer struggle to get along.

When I got to the house, the body was gone. One of the family members had decided it was best for me to not see her, and for some reason that made me angry. Daddy said he'd run into a friend at the grocery store who had recently lost her husband. "EJ," the friend said to my dad, "I realized my prayers had been holding my husband here. You may need to release Judy." Daddy said when he got home he sat by Momma and said, "Father if I have been keeping her here, I release her to you." As he finished his prayer, the phone rang and he left her side to answer it. The caller was a concerned friend (I was always surprised at how many friends my momma had because we just didn't have that kind of relationship) calling for an update on Momma's condition and Daddy's mental state. After ten minutes on the phone, relaying Momma's condition for what must have been the hundredth time that day, Daddy hung up the phone, walked back into the living room, and Momma was gone.

Momma died on JoJo's first day of kindergarten and two days later, we buried her on his fifth birthday. Charlie was not quite three. Friends of Joe's and mine took care of the boys. The night of her wake, over 400 people came to the viewing. The funeral home thought there was a dignitary there, but it was just Momma. She was loved by so many, a fact that only made me feel that much worse about my relationship with her.

The day of her funeral was bright and sunny. As we walked to the burial site, I remembered thinking it was Jojo's birthday and every year since the year he'd been born the weather was beautiful for his birthday. The evening of the funeral, the ladies of the church brought our family food. My next-door neighbor had baked a birthday cake for JoJo and took me to buy a gift for him. We had plenty friends and family over, and JoJo thought it was his birthday party. I didn't tell the boys she died until the day after the funeral. I didn't want JoJo to equate his birthday with the death of his grandmother.

Chapter Ten
REALITY SETS IN

Three months after mom's death, Dad started dating and just nine months after her death, he remarried. The suddenness with which he replaced my mother stunned me, but I heard from many people that his reaction was not all that uncommon.

I had slipped into the familiar dark hole of depression, crying that first year, mostly at the guilt and regret of not being able to mend fences with my mom before she died. Mom and I did not get along, but I missed the idealism of having a nurturing mother. I don't mean that I longed for a mom who was physically affectionate. Mom, her mom, her grandmother, and the aunts were not very huggy, kissy, but that was the personality of our Italian family. I just wanted her to nurture me and show her affection for me in the same way she showed others. For example, when my sister-in-law had a baby, my mom took her breakfast every single day. I said to her one day, "Mom, why don't you come see me and JoJo anymore?" She replied, "Because you don't need me, Lisa. She needs me." But that was not the truth. I did need her. Just because I was independent didn't mean I didn't love or need my mother.

The reality of "no mom" had settled in, and I was in a very dark place. Mom would forever be a memory with no more opportunity to fix our relationship. My house was a mess. I hadn't touched the mail and had received notice that they were going to turn off my water. My friend came by to get me out of the house. I told her what I really wanted was for her to take the boys for the day so I could catch up on the mail and get my house in order. For a long time after Momma's death, I battled depression and anxiety. On days I couldn't cope, I climbed into my bed and told my boys that momma was taking a happy nap. Usually when I got up, I felt better. I hated that part about myself because people viewed me as happy and bubbly, but that was not me, not then at least. I had so many insecurities I was trying to hide. But I think more than anything else, I was overwhelmed with guilt over the condition of the relationship I had with my mom. I loved her and at the same time, I didn't like her. I wish I had a mom now. Most importantly, I wish I had made peace with her.

As a personal organizer, I learned that sometimes the circumstances of our life can turn even the most organized person into a cluttered mess. The source of my mess was not a lack of organizational skills. It was because my mother died and turned my world upside down in the process.

Katrina's Story – A Storm of A Different Making

One day the phone rang. I was expecting a call from my sister, so I didn't pay attention to the caller ID and answered the phone, "Hello Darling." The caller said, "I'll be your darling," causing me to look down quickly at the caller ID. Much to my embarrassment, I realized it was most certainly NOT my sister. I apologized profusely, but I believe my blunder opened a door for Katrina and I to become fast friends.

When I arrived at Katrina's home, she answered the door with no makeup, her hair pulled back, and a warm welcoming smile on her face. The first floor of the home was exactly as I expected, fabulous. Everything was beautifully decorated and in order. As we went upstairs to the second floor, I started to notice the telltale signs. There were toys and clothes scattered on the staircase and floor. I felt a little bit like a detective who'd discovered her first clue.

In another part of the home, I was drawn into the conversation and laughter of other women. Funny how the media portrays the ball players and their families in such a different light and here they were studying the Word of God and sharing their hearts together. I can tell you I certainly didn't expect to find that.

During our assessment time, I discovered that due to the traveling schedule of her husband; Katrina wanted nothing more than to create a sense of order and stability for their children, sheltering them from the storm that comes with living such a public and ever-changing life. Katrina was getting ready to have baby number 3 and wanted to get the nursery in order. We continued the organizing process in the children's rooms, rooms to be the constant for their lives.

What a good mom. What a warm and loving mom to understand that her children needed stability to feel secure. Though her home was certainly anything but cluttered, she was very proactive in keeping in that way. Sometimes it's important to remember that constantly purging our closets (and our minds) is a great way to prevent clutter in the first place.

Chapter Eleven
A NEW LIGHT

The year after mom died, Joe and I changed churches. I wanted to be at a church that was close to home where my boys could be involved, and the church had a private school where my boys attended. There were so many great women there that I connected with. I can honestly say that change probably saved my life.

I met Debra Schaefer when JoJo was a baby. She took care of him in daycare when I worked temporary jobs. That is when Debra and I became best friends. I believe God promises that he won't give us more than we can handle and he knew it was time for Debra to come into my life to soothe my hurts and bring some laughter. And he knew I needed the validation of a close friendship.

When my momma passed, Debra's family became my family, and her mother-in-law "Mamaw Dot" as we called her, became like a mom to me. Joe would say to her, "Did I kiss you today?" She always smiled and said, "No you didn't," and he would kiss her. She was special to all of us. She supported me, cheered me on, and helped me out of my hole. She was huggy, kissy, and lots of fun to be around. It was difficult raising children without a mom to help. I so wanted my boys to have their grandmother. In the most loving way possible, Debra's family helped to fill in the holes that I felt were missing in my life.

Debra and I supported one another in so many ways. There were times when Debra needed money for a prescription for her children, and I gave it to her. And then there were times when I needed grocery money, and she took care of it for me. I loved having a clean kitchen but Debra hated doing dishes. Debra never wanted clothes to sit in the dryer and get wrinkled, but I didn't care about wrinkles as long as the clothes were clean.

Our solution was I did her dishes and she did my laundry. What a great friendship! When Debra's husband went hunting, she stayed at my house. She called my guest bedroom her room. It was like a slumber party. Anytime she slept at my house, we chatted and giggled like little girls. We always said of our friendship, "we don't keep score we just keep each other."

When we were having mommy burnout moments, we traded kids. (That was fun and a good break.) Debra lived close to our kids' school, so in the mornings after Debra and I dropped the kids off at school, we went back to her house and had our devotions together. That time was so special to us both. It's when we shared our prayer requests and rejoiced at our answered prayers together. Debra was the symbol of unconditional friendship, support, and love. Every young mom, especially one without a mom, needs a friend like Debra.

One of the best things about Debra was she didn't judge me for being loud or liking to organize things. She was just as loud as I was. And if she called and asked what I was doing and I "happened" to be cleaning out a closet, she'd tease me mercilessly and say, "You need to get a life." But with Debra, I always knew that teasing was in love. We loved to tease one another and help each other.

My family still gave me a hard time with wanting things to be organized though. But my friends knew I liked to organize, and they not only liked that, they wanted me to help them. Anytime someone needed organizing, they called me. I loved the very process of putting things in order. It was what I could control in my life.

One day as I was flipping through cable TV I came across an organizing show and I thought to myself, "I could totally do that!" I asked a relative to help me set up a website so that I could have an organizing club to help people. Once again, I was told, "Who would want that?" My love of organizing never faded and neither did my dream of having a business. Debra and I were dreamers, and we encouraged that in each other. Her dream was a blue vacation to a tropical island and mine was starting a business. Even our dreams reflected how different we were, and yet we were best friends. I encouraged her desire to get away, and she encouraged my desire to make something different out of my life.

Janine's Story – Making Up For Lost Time

Janine was a lively and vivacious woman. She loved to talk and engage you in conversation. She wore plenty of makeup, lots of jewelry, and her clothes were very bright and colorful. Her home was decorated elaborately. Most of the walls and flat surfaces in her home were filled with art, curios, flowers, and such. Everything about her said, "Excess."

Growing up in a conservative home, Janine was not permitted to wear fancy clothes or jewelry. When she got married, her motto was to catch up on lost time. She wanted to surround herself with beautiful clothes and accessories. And boy did she.

Janine worked full-time and loved to use her money to buy things that made her happy. The only problem for Janine was the things she thought would make her happy, weren't making her happy. Her "stuff" was wreaking havoc in her life to say the least. Another concern she had was that there was no closet in the office and her paperwork and office supplies were not pretty to display. She wanted all the rooms in her home to look pretty, even her office.

Sometimes too many items turn into clutter that you are unable to enjoy. And that was definitely the case with Janine. She wasn't willing to release any of her pretty clothes, shoes, purses, jewelry, or other items. But as always, when you are organizing clutter, there are usually just a couple of choices: purge some of your things or add storage space.

Janine went for shelving in her closets. Cute and functional containers in the office armoire provided storage for paperwork and office supplies. Her home turned out beautiful.

At the end of the day, I realized that Janine was like so many of my other clients, and so much like me. Her clutter came from a reactive response to something she felt she'd been denied in childhood. Had she been able to make peace with those feelings, she might have more easily been able to purge, and possibly even reduce her need for more.

Chapter Twelve

TONE IT DOWN GIRLS

I spent most of my boys' elementary years working part-time at our church. It helped financially, and I enjoyed being with and teaching the preschoolers. But my passion was organizing and training the volunteers and encouraging all the people. Debra and I both loved working in Children's Church. We had so much fun playing with the children and creating fun games and activities. We were like kids ourselves.

Debra and I didn't hold anything back, and we enjoyed life. Our supervisor often got after Debra and me saying we were acting unprofessional. She said we were too boisterous and needed to tone down our mannerisms (whatever THAT meant)! It didn't bother Debra in the least, but it bothered me. I had over 70 volunteers under me. There were so many women that I was reaching out to. One husband even said to me that when they had first moved to our community, his wife had recently lost a baby, and my reaching out to her had made all the difference.

Finally, after so many years of not being myself, I finally felt free to live, and laugh, and love. And here, once again was someone telling me to be something different. I knew I was probably being overly sensitive to the remark about my behavior, but I knew I was helping many people. I decided to go to school and get my Bible degree thinking maybe that would help me be more professional. That'd show her!

All kidding aside, at least I'd come out with my education, something I'd always wanted to accomplish and finally did.

Anna's Story – Anna Meets The 21st Century

Anna was a warm and friendly woman who owned a banquet hall and catering company for many years. She was dressed very casually, which matched her very casual and approachable personality. Her business was a household name in the community. She said to me "Lisa, my messy office never seemed to bother me, but I started wondering why I was not making more money. I am getting new customers all the time," she said. She then continued the conversation by saying, "I started looking through old files and realized that I had forgotten to bid on certain big events. I assumed I would always get the job. Now I see there are new caterers in town and they are serving my customers. I need to get organized and try to get them back."

I told Anna, "In addition to getting your office organized, we need to set you up with a plan and schedule the time to track and bid on these annual events, but also to visit and win over your long time customers. Times have changed and the way we used to do things sometimes no longer works. You have to be open to new things and new ideas."

For Anna, it was a process of reacquainting herself with her customers and learning to do business in the 21st century. Not only did this put Anna in the right direction, but it also gave her the opportunity to launch the next phase in her company.

Sometimes we are so used to doing things our old way, even reacting in old familiar patterns that we miss opportunities that are right in front of us. Uncluttering life isn't always about cleaning up our messes, but about embracing new ways to accomplish life.

Chapter Thirteen
THE GREAT TRANSITION

In 1998, Joe and I moved into our dream home. It was in a gated community overlooking the golf course. We had a beautiful L-shaped front porch with a back screened-in porch and atrium room. I guess technically it was Joe's dream home. I had been content in my little house, but it was so nice to see Joe happy. We lived next door to our friends, and we had the party house.

Joe and I lived within six miles of my childhood home and in the same geographical area where I went to school. I loved my community. Everywhere I went, I ran into at least two or three people that I knew. One evening after a Bible study, Joe and I were in separate cars, I told him I needed to pick up a few things at the grocery store. An hour and a half later, I returned home to a frazzled and frantic husband. "Where have you been?" he demanded. "I have been worried sick. I almost called the police looking for you!" I felt bad that he was so worried, but I couldn't help but giggle a little when I answered. "I saw Trudy and started chatting. I guess time got away and then I thought I would just do big groceries, besides you never tell me where you are going." The next day, Joe bought me a cell phone. One of my friends called it an electronic leash; funny how times have changed.

In 1999, the economy took a tumble and so did Joe's salary. We could no longer afford our dream home, but the market became upside down and selling was not an option. On the outside, we were living the dream, but on the inside, we were fighting to stay afloat. We were $54,000 in credit card debt.

My husband's company transferred us from New Orleans to Houston in 2003. I left kicking and screaming, but we needed to go where the work was. I was very lonely in Houston. The culture was very different to me. New Orleans had such a party atmosphere and a place where I knew so many people. I had spent the majority of my life in the same six-mile radius, and now I felt like an outsider. Many of the women I met in Houston had either grown up together or had raised their children together. I was not invited to their gatherings. I continued with getting my education and settled back in to the role of stay-at-home wife and now homeschool mom.

Of course, Debra and I remained close even though we lived almost 400 miles away from each other. We talked on the phone a couple of times a day sharing our adventures. Every two months, I took a road trip to New Orleans with my boys to visit friends, but mostly Debra. I loved my community. I loved that I knew so many people. I had loved having big parties on a regular basis. It's fun to be popular and have the party home. I am definitely an extrovert who thrives on crowds. But moving to Houston, Texas, was a culture and lifestyle shock. I knew no one and the worst part was once I began to meet people they didn't always understand the culture and lifestyle that I had come from. We had no history together like I did with the people in New Orleans. It was difficult to make friends, which was very upsetting to me. I was consumed with the thought of getting money and getting back home to New Orleans.

My only survival was my regular trips and daily calls to Debra. I loved that girl; she was my best friend forever. The school year before we moved, my oldest announced he was quitting school in 8th grade. JoJo had struggled with ADHD and the private school didn't have the resources to accommodate him. I was frustrated at paying so much money for a private education to come home to three hours of homework. It didn't make sense. I had a couple of friends who were homeschooling successfully. So, I sought their wisdom, did plenty of research, and decided this would be best for my family. Debra had also homeschooled her children as well, which was how I was able to visit her so often after we moved. Thank goodness, it was only a six-hour drive.

Candy's Story – A Horse of A Different Color

I met with Candy at a Starbucks in an upscale part of town. Candy was meticulously dressed in a designer outfit, hair, and fancy nails to boot. She had an oversized matching purse next to her feet as she sat in the overstuffed chair. As we began to discuss organizing she leaned forward and said, "Can you organize my life?" That was during my first year in business, and it really caught me off guard, but it was the beginning of my journey in how I help people organize the big picture in their life.

Candy proceeded to tell me her story. She came from an affluent home in another state. She was a trust fund baby and socialite and didn't hold a traditional job. Candy lived the perfect life to most people. She married David, a very handsome and charming man. He knew how to influence people. He proceeded to take her inheritance and quickly became a successful real estate investor. He moved about the community with his charm. Everyone thought David was wonderful. But David had a secret life.

After ten years of marriage and two children, David began drinking. One day, Candy received a startling phone call from a mutual friend. The man on the phone was distraught as he exclaimed to David's wife, "I believe David is cheating on me." The words hit her hard. Was this man telling her that he was having an affair with her husband? She dropped to the chair in her kitchen, still holding the receiver to her ear. How could her husband be living a homosexual lifestyle?

Of course David denied it. And Candy, not wanting to bring shame to her family, chose to hide his secret. She thought that maybe she did something wrong as a wife.

As time went on, she became depressed and her doctor put her on an antidepressant. When Candy could no longer hold the secret in, she told her family, but her family refused to believe the news. What a double betrayal. David then used the fact that she was on antidepressants to prove to her family she was crazy. David didn't want to lose his status in the community or her family's money. Feeling like she was losing her mind, Candy came to Houston to stay with a brother until she could come up with a plan. Candy wanted assistance in organizing and moving her furniture out of the family home and starting a new life.

As Candy unfolded her story, I sat there in unbelief. I thought that perhaps she was making it all up. I went home to do research on the computer about her story, and sure enough, it was all true. (It's amazing what all you can find out on the Internet!) I just needed to figure out the best way to help her.

It's certainly easy to *want* to ignore things that are too hard or too messy to deal with, but sometimes the direct approach is the best approach. For Candy, David's cluttered life had become hers. She found her strength and purpose when she moved out from under the cloud of David's secret. For many of us, we are living in the middle of someone else's messy life. The answer isn't always leaving. But recognizing that the mess we are in might actually be someone else's mess can be the first step toward finding the strength we need.

Chapter Fourteen

WHEN THE WATERS RISE

In August 2005, just two years after we moved to Houston, Hurricane Katrina hit and devastated New Orleans. The morning that the storm hit, we watched the news in horror as the roof was being torn off the Superdome, the waters rising, and bodies floating. My husband and I took care of 28 people and helped them to get situated. We physically had a family of five living with us. I spent several weeks with little food or sleep, surviving on coffee with countless hours on the phone coordinating efforts to get friends back in the city. I was exhausted and ended up in the emergency room with chest pains.

After one month, the city gave clearance for people to begin returning home. The homeschool community in Houston and my church friends gathered around me during this time to help me help my New Orleans friends. I couldn't have done it without their help. Debra rode out Katrina in a hunting camp in Mississippi, but when she returned to New Orleans, she found life very difficult. She asked to live with me, but at the time, I was caring for 28 people and couldn't handle anyone else, especially since she had a 21-month-old baby.

By November, two months after Katrina, I had planned my first trip to see Debra. On Thursday, November 3rd, Debra called crying and saying, "I need you to come now; things are so hard." I said, "Deb, I'll be there next Wednesday. That's less than a week away." Debra never cried. She was always optimistic, even when she was upset or annoyed, so I was very, very worried.

Sunday night, November 6th, Joe and I arrived at 6:00 for our Sunday night Bible study at my friend Sonya's house. At 6:35, I leaned over and told Joe "I don't feel good, I need to leave." He replied, "What are you talking about, we just got here?" Ten minutes later, I received the phone call. The caller said, "Please pray. Debra has been in an accident and her head has been hit." Interesting how something in my spirit sensed something was wrong.

Three months earlier, I had a dream that Joe was driving, and I was killed in a car accident. I wish I had prayed then. Looking back, I wondered if it was Debra in my dreams, and if I had prayed that night, would she still be alive? Debra's in-laws had lost three houses and were going to check on a forth property when the accident happened. They were driving on the old Highway 11 bridge because the Causeway and the Twin Spans had been damaged during the storm. A pickup truck was traveling in the opposite direction and didn't have his boat trailer secured. It came undone and air born. The coupler came through the windshield and hit her in the head. Joe and I quickly left the Bible study to make phone calls to Debra's family to find out what was going on. My sons were receiving conflicting calls as to her status. One call said, "She's gone."

I couldn't sleep that night and by morning, I was a wreck. Joe had left for work, and I tried to accomplish a few things around the house, but I couldn't concentrate not knowing what was going on. I called Joe and said, "I'm going to see her." Joe said, "Wait for me, I'm coming home now to take you." Nothing prepared me for the devastation I saw in New Orleans. I felt like I was going to throw up. Everything was gray except for the buildings covered with blue roofs. There were red circles with X's on the front doors with dates and numbers denoting body counts and such. It looked like a war zone. I asked Joe to pull off the interstate so I could get a cup of coffee. So much was destroyed. We found one place opened, but it was crawling with military people and guns to keep order. I burst into tears. "This is the United States!" I thought. It was so surreal. There were only a couple of places to get food to eat and no hotels. Everything shut down at dark. We were able to buy a couple of sandwiches at a gas station. Joe and I slept at the hospital and in our vehicle.

Debra was on life support. We went home a couple of days later, and the following week I received the call. "Debra has passed, I'm so sorry Lisa." When I returned for the funeral, the picture they used was the one of Debra and me on my sofa. I had been Photoshopped out. What an eerie feeling that was. Her mom and mother-in-law had lost all of their photos in the floodwaters of Katrina. I spoke at her funeral because everyone knew how close we were. One of my friends said, "I was waiting for you to cry and knew I wouldn't be able to hold it together." But I didn't cry. I don't know how or why, but I didn't.

The following year is still a blur to me. To say that Katrina was a life changing event would be an understatement. To personally watch your childhood home be devastated is horrible. I felt the pain that all my friends were feeling as well. I desperately wanted to help everyone get on their feet. I am a server and giver. I am a fixer and this was an area I couldn't fix.

Not surprisingly, I blamed myself for Debra's death. Maybe if I had let her live with me, she would still be alive. There was consolation in how appreciative everyone was to the things I was able to do for them, but I didn't help Debra. And to know that the accident occurred just when I was about to go visit her . . . the shock and grief of Debra's death was too much to deal with.

Most people thought that when the storm passed and the water subsided that it was safe to return. The news didn't report how many people were killed in vehicle accidents. My world as I knew it was over. Debra was like a soulmate. At times, I felt closer to her than my husband. Girls love to share their hearts, dreams, giggles, and secrets. What do you do when someone who is part of your world is suddenly gone? I felt lost. I couldn't function, but I had a family, and I had to pick myself up and go on. Debra was truly my best friend, the first person I ever felt that loved me for who I was; and she was gone.

Sharon's Story – One Tough Cookie

Sharon was the owner of a design firm with five employees. She was incredibly talented and creative in the way she decorated a home. "It gives me great pleasure to watch someone be excited with the outcome," she said. " I love making them feel happy."

Sharon was dressed in designer jeans and a cute top. Her mannerism was very warm, but I could see she was a tough businesswoman. "I need a lot of help organizing. I'm embarrassed, Lisa." During the first hour of organizing, she abruptly left the project with an employee. When the organizing was complete, I sent her a text with a picture of the closet. She was excited and scheduled our next appointment. We continued organizing various areas of her shop and home. There was a pattern of her abruptly leaving or making sharp remarks that bothered me.

One day she confided, "My youngest child died in a car accident when she was only eight years old. If only I had not let her go to the movies that day with her friend. I wasn't there for her." Finally, I understood her erratic behavior. She'd spent her life helping others, and in the hour she was needed most, she hadn't been there. She helped others, but didn't feel she deserved help; so letting me help her get control of her life was definitely taking an emotional toll.

Getting organized helped her to find a sense of order and control in her life. It was fun watching her lighten up and have a smile on her face. She was a work in progress for sure. I totally get it, Sharon. I totally get it.

Chapter Fifteen
PICKING UP THE PIECES

Two years after Debra's death, I completed my Bible degree. It wasn't that the degree was that important to me, but my life was sinking in sadness, and I needed to accomplish something. Debra died, and I wasn't there for her, and moving on from that felt insurmountable at times. Each morning, armed with a new resolve, I worked on my degree and cleaned and organized things (I'm a stress organizer). But by each afternoon, I was on the sofa again, sitting, sad, and unsure how to move forward.

Once I completed my degree, I decided to get busy figuring out how to use it. When Joe and I first moved to Houston, we found a church, and got busy volunteering. I had been serving as a volunteer staff member there so when we were invited by a church in a neighboring community to attend a church leadership conference, I jumped at the chance. While attending one of the workshops at the conference, a woman from Oklahoma (a stranger to me) said, "God said to tell you your ministry is not within the four walls of the church and you might miss it if I don't tell you twice because you are not looking for it." Anytime someone starts a sentence with "God said to tell you . . ." I am immediately on guard. But this woman's statement was doubly troubling. I had no clue what the woman was trying to tell me, but I thought certainly she had heard God incorrectly. I most certainly knew God was telling me to work for him, and it just didn't make sense to me that it would be anywhere else but a church.

But the seed was planted in my brain, and I could not stop thinking about her words. "God said to tell you your ministry is not within the four walls of the church."

The next morning, I woke up at 4:00 a.m. and started feverishly writing notes on organizing. Joe woke up at 5:00 a.m., saw me writing notes like a mad woman and asked, "What are you doing?" "I don't know," I replied, "but I think God wants me to do something with organizing." Joe looked at me sitting in the dim light of my bedside lamp, shook his head (I'm sure trying to wrap his head around what in the world I was doing), and had the good sense to roll over and go back to sleep.

Later that week, I called my friend, Brenda, and told her what had happened in those early morning hours. "I think I am supposed to do something with organizing," I said. "Does that make any sense? What could that be?" Brenda looked at me and smiled and said, "Lisa, my daughter, Sally, is a professional organizer."

"Are you kidding?" I asked. "People really do that as a business? I thought that was only on TV!" But she wasn't kidding, and I couldn't get the thought out of my head.

I began my quest for setting up a business. I didn't have a clue what I needed to do, so I talked to everyone that I could. A couple of months later, I mentioned to my banker that I wanted to start an organizing business and didn't know how. She said to me, "Lisa, I have this women's lunch meeting I want you to come to." Now, she was a Louisiana girl as well and she went on to say, "This is not like a New Orleans lunch meeting." I was in shock at my first meeting. I didn't realize there were so many businesswomen out there, nor did I realize they got together for lunch to help each other and talk business. An interior designer there came up to me after the meeting and said, "Have you considered joining the National Association of Professional Organizers?" I went home and searched online for the local chapter. It was past the deadline to register for the April meeting, but I begged them to let me attend. I had already registered my business name, but joining their organization was the moment that I felt like I launched my business.

Within a week, I had my first paid organizing job. The first few years in business were totally exciting as I moved about the community. I saw the opportunity, and the sky was the limit. I wasn't just walking through open doors; I was running through them. They were everywhere. I was doing everything I had dreamed of as a girl; the galas, working with politicians, sports and TV figures, and successful business people. I had published an award-winning book on organizing; I was speaking at events, making TV appearances and best of all I had built a thriving, growing business. In the midst of all of that, I received my credentials as a licensed minister and became a volunteer staff member to a ministry in Washington, D.C. My world felt perfect.

I still missed Debra and longed for that kind of friendship again. In truth, there would never be another Debra, but it took me a long time to figure that out. I discovered a lot about myself in the years after her death though, and perhaps the biggest thing of all was discovering I had ideas and opinions that mattered to people. I was a well-respected businesswoman and people sought my help, important people.

Yet somewhere in the back of my mind was this nagging thought; why in the world had God called me to become a licensed minister if He wanted me to be a professional organizer? At times, I felt that God gave me my business to save me from the despair I faced in relocating to Houston and then in losing Debra. For the first time in a very long time, I felt an excitement and purpose in my life. I was elated at the possibilities and opportunities that were in front of me.

It took me five years to both find myself and piece my life back together after moving to Houston. With every single woman and family I helped, I knew that I was fulfilling my ministry outside the four walls of the church.

Nancy – Discovering Why

On the outside, Nancy had the ideal life. Her husband, Paul was a successful business man in the city with over 200 employees, they had two wonderful sons; one was an excellent ball player and the other an academic genius. They owned a large home, a vacation home, and she was active in volunteering in her community. Nancy also attended to some of the company's administrative duties from her home office. She called me up because her husband complained that the house was a mess. Interestingly enough, she had a full-time housekeeper, but the closets and her home office were a mess. Most people do not realize that housekeeping and organizing are not the same and housekeepers are not always organized. Some housekeepers shove stuff into drawers, cabinets, and closets, or they just dust around piles.

As we began to work together, she confided to me "Lisa, I am so depressed some days I can't even get out of bed. Paul is always so critical of me, I feel like I can't do anything right, and so I've just adopted the motto of "Why bother trying to organize?"

After working with Nancy for two months, we finally got her house in order. We were now on a maintenance plan for her to keep things organized. Periodically, I'd check in just to be sure things were staying organized, according to her plan. A couple of months went by before I got back to her house to check on things. There was some maintenance work I needed to do, so I didn't see Nancy. In fact, it was odd that she stayed locked away most of the time. I could tell that for some reason, she was avoiding me.

When everyone had left, she came out. I looked at her and said, "You're avoiding me, for some reason, but I'm praying for you anyway." She grabbed me and hugged me and said, "I need you, Lisa. We need to talk." We set a time to talk privately and when we met, she confided in me some deep concerns she had in her marriage and with the children. I grabbed her hand, listened to her, and guided her to resources to assist her.

The mantra of organizers is that when you are organized, you feel better about yourself and your life. While this is true, I have learned that helping women discover why their life got messy to begin with is a much bigger and more important aspect of what I do. I'm part organizer and part counselor. I now know why God wanted me to be a minister.

I set up a maintenance plan for Nancy that we still work on today, but mostly we developed a mutual trust and friendship. If I don't hear from her for a while, I send a text or voicemail letting her know I am still here. She tells me "Thank you for checking on me, even if I don't answer right away."

Chapter Sixteen

A SAFE
DISTANCE

Have you ever seen those signs that say, "If Mama ain't happy, ain't nobody happy." Well let me just tell you, that is 100% total truth. 2013 will go down in my history as the year of "M"; May, money, memories, and menopause. And let me just tell you, it's a miracle any of us survived it. For the men in my life, "M" stood for "Every Man for himself!"

I like to blame menopause for the upheaval of my emotions and my life that year. (That's my story, and I'm sticking to it!) But according to my doctor, I was the perfect storm waiting to happen; insomnia, menopause, and the stress of running a business all colliding in a swirling sea of madness, just waiting for the right moment to make landfall.

It was January of 2013, almost eight years since Debra's death, and I was going a million miles an hour. Sitting on top of the world professionally, I was living my dream, though truthfully I was too busy to really enjoy it. I was also going through menopause and insomnia, a combination that proved to be my undoing. I didn't have insomnia as in "I couldn't fall asleep" insomnia. Falling asleep wasn't a problem at all. It was staying asleep that was the trouble for me. I'd fall asleep for a few hours and then wake up and stay awake for hours on end. Not wanting to waste time (I mean, after all, I'm an organizational guru, an efficiency expert) I would get on my computer to work since I was awake anyway. Sometimes I'd be able to fall back asleep for a couple of hours, but then I would launch my day at full speed.

I was glad for the occasional nap, but in truth, I was not getting everything done. There was no time for cooking or taking care of my home responsibilities. I was so glad that my sons still lived at home because they sure picked up my slack with grocery shopping, cooking, dishes, laundry, and errands. My business was beyond booming; more paid speaking offers were coming in as were more TV appearance offers. And if that wasn't enough, I was just about ready to launch a product line.

I loved the work I was doing. I loved the intimate conversations that I had with my clients and the connections we made. My work as a minister and my theology background allowed me to really reach into their lives. It was fulfilling that they opened up their hearts and shared their lives with me. It was incredible to be able to love on them and encourage them. I wanted to be a total solution in their lives. They may have called about wanting to organize a cluttered closet or office, but it became much more.

And while I loved the relationship I had with my clients, I still had not yet found someone that I could be myself with, a close personal friendship like the one I'd had with Debra.

I had a business acquaintance named Leslie. She was going to a conference, and I asked to attend with her. "Lisa, I'm not going to be able to socialize with you, I need to get work done while I am there." That was fine to me. I'm not shy I can always find someone to talk to. "Oh, by the way, I invited Rebecca to go with us; I think you've met her before." Leslie continued.

The second day of the event, I had lunch with Rebecca. We became fast friends, with much in common. She was easy to talk to and made me laugh, something I had not done much of since the death of Debra. She was a successful businesswoman and became a cheerleader to what I was doing. She showed compassion and helped me in my business when I needed it. We just connected on so many levels.

Rebecca was fun, and being a New Orleans girl, fun was something I had been missing. Where I had stepped away from business network meetings for a while, Rebecca brought me back into the business social circles and man did that girl know how to have fun.

Someone said years ago, "The same wall you use to protect yourself also keeps people out." I needed to let someone in, to stand with me, someone who understood not only Lisa Giesler as a wife, mom, and a woman, but as a business owner. One day Rebecca picked me up to have lunch together. It was lots of fun giggling and sharing secrets. When she dropped me off she went to give me a hug goodbye, but I pulled away. "What's the matter?" Rebecca asked. "Nothing," I replied. "Well hug me!" she insisted. I put my purse down and she gave me a huge bear hug. It felt very unnerving. You see, I didn't let anyone hug me because hugging meant I had I let you into my inner circle. I didn't let people into my inner circle because when I did, they hurt me, they rejected me, or they died.

I realized I had a void, a giant gap left by a lifetime of my father's callous remarks, my mother's rejection and Debra's death. The upheaval of my emotional state in those previous few months could no longer be ignored. Rebecca's simple gesture of a hug had destroyed the walls around my heart and mind. I couldn't pretend it didn't matter any more.

In church one evening, at a ladies meeting, the Women's Director announced the new book we would go through together for small group devotions. She read an excerpt of one of the chapters in the book. The chapter she read addressed how women feel about themselves, their lives, and God. I became flooded with so many memories that I had not even realized were there. I came face to face with the memories of my past, the death of my mom and Debra. I began to sob as I thought about the loss and regrets. "Great. How do you deal with the past when they are dead?" I asked the Women's Director. I viewed myself as a tough and independent person and now I was angry with myself for feeling emotional all the time and for not feeling very confident.

By the end of March, I felt like my world was tumbling. At some point, I realized I wasn't as organized as usual. Normally, when life gets a little off track, I can quickly get myself reorganized. But that was not the case this time. I seemed to be having a more difficult time getting myself together. One morning, as I was getting dressed, I looked at myself in the mirror and said, "Lisa Giesler, You are almost 51 years old. You run your own business, and you have a Type-A personality. What in the world is happening to you? Look at yourself. You are usually helping others heal and move forward with their life. But look at yourself. You are a mess. Your house is a mess and your life is a mess." I couldn't concentrate on my bookkeeping, my marketing, or other business administrative duties. Things were getting behind and I could see it, but I had a hard time reining it in. My business was starting to suffer.

I attended my women's small group (though truthfully I dreaded it), and we started the first chapter of our study together. That first chapter really hit a nerve. After everyone was gone, and I was cleaning things up, I was fighting back the feeling of crying. I could barely speak. "What is wrong?" Rebecca asked. "You can share it with me, Lisa. You can trust me." I shared my despair at the loss of Debra. I went on to say, "Part of me wanted a close friend like Debra, and the other part was afraid of getting too close. If you don't get close to someone, then you can't lose them." She made me feel better by saying, "Had you never lost Debra, you may not have started your business. Think of all the people you have helped."

An interesting thing that I discovered during that time; I began using my monthly newsletter, which had been used for organizing tips, as a type of reflective and lamenting blog sharing all my faults and struggles. My readers loved it. The women began responding with comments such as; "Thank you for sharing that." I asked Rebecca why she thought people liked hearing that my house and my life were a mess. She said, "People like to know you are real, Lisa, so they can relate to you. I like knowing you are not perfect."

She was right. Unless you walk in someone's shoes, you really can't relate. Up to that point in my life, I had always counted on perfectionism, legalism, and fake smiles to keep my life together. I didn't like feeling out of control, but I was definitely learning to relate to the women God was bringing into my life.

There was something about my friendship with Rebecca that I couldn't explain. She was the first person I felt connected to since Debra's death. There are friends and then there are close friends. It seems like there are different levels of friendship for the different parts of our lives, and I felt that Rebecca was definitely in my life for a reason.

In April, I went to New Orleans for the National Association of Professional Organizers annual conference. I made sure I took time to visit friends while I was there, thinking it would help my mental state. It was great seeing old friends. I loved being able to pick up where we left off and spending time laughing and sharing our lives. Before I returned to Houston, I visited mom's grave. I was surprised that I still felt sad and angry. I talked to her and sobbed. It was the first time I had visited her grave in many years. I knew she wasn't there, but it was a connecting place.

Monique – Behind Closed Doors

Monique was a funny woman. Her house was a mess, but she seemed engaged with our conversation. "My husband works for an oil company and moved us to Houston five years ago. But when it was time to move to the Middle East, my sons said, No," she said matter-of-factly. "It is very difficult to make friends and then to leave. My boys are teens and this is where they want to make their roots."

She proceeded to guide me through her home and show me photos of the family and all their travels. "My husband is coming home for the holidays, and I want the house ready." The first organizing appointment was the front formal room. It had been the dumping room for all things misplaced. We created an inviting dining room for the family, and it felt good to bring a sense of order to at least one room in the house.

It was the first of November, and I was due to return the following week, when I received an email from Monique saying for me not to come. Her husband came home unexpectedly, and she needed to focus on him. The first of December I received a call from Monique saying, "I really need you to help me."

When I arrived at her home, Monique was very depressed. "Walter came home and was unusually quiet and moody. I tried to talk to him and all he could say was, 'Work is stressful.' By the second week, he admitted he was having an affair. What am I going to do?" she cried. She said, "You realize I don't have anyone else to listen to me? The marriage has been in trouble for many years. I have been so depressed, and that's why my house is a mess. My family lives up northeast, and I am so lonely." Boy could I relate.

"I am here to assist in any way I can," I said. Two days later, I received a call from Monique, "I don't feel like living," she whispered into the phone. "I want to kill myself," she said. I quickly called her teenage son so that we could help her. Her son had her hospitalized. Two weeks later Monique called to say she was home. "Thank you for helping me, but I will no longer need your services," she said. The family moved shortly thereafter, and I lost touch with her. I think of her often, hoping she is ok.

A SAFE DISTANCE

We cannot always recognize the clutter and chaos of someone else's life. My first impression was a happy woman with a hard working husband and three great teenagers. Stresses in life can cause depression and a feeling of hopelessness. I was glad to be there for her during that time in her life. I miss you Monique. If you find this story and can tell it's you, I'd love to hear from you.

Chapter Seventeen
MAY MADNESS

I love celebrating my birthday. It's the one time of the year where it is all about me. When May 15th rolls around, I can count on the universe taking note that it is MY DAY. When Debra was alive, I would laugh and say, "Can't you sense it in the universe, Debra, it's almost our birthday?" We didn't technically share our birthday. Debra's birthday was May 28th. But every year for our birthday, we spent the day together shopping and going out to eat. No one was permitted to join us, though occasionally one of her sister-in-laws would want to come. To be nice, we'd let them come, but they had to abide by our rule. The rule was "If you want to come, you have to buy lunch and buy us a present."

Debra's and my motto on gifts were the same. "No surprises, buy me what I want." When I found the exact gift I wanted, I handed it to Debra, and she bought it. Then she'd turn around and give to me excitedly saying, "Happy Birthday, Lisa!" And my gift giving to her looked the same. It was so much fun. The Mays following her death were extremely hard. Not only did I miss our birthday celebration together, but I also had to face Mother's Day without a mother and with a lot of unresolved emotions related to her.

When I was a newly married adult, one Mother's Day our church hosted a mother-daughter luncheon. There was a PowerPoint presentation where certain of the leadership of the church gushed over their moms and all the wonderful things they did for them. I remember sitting there feeling angry, guilty, and frustrated that I did not have those feelings or wonderful memories. I just had to endure the presentation. I had enough friends in my life at the time that I didn't dwell on the negative, I just moved on.

After mom died, Joe and I celebrated Mother's Day each year with one of my friends' family. They were a large family and always had a big barbecue. Plus, I had Debra and her family was my family. But when Debra died, I was alone in Houston without family and close friends; I simply didn't acknowledge Mother's Day at all.

In May of 2013, I began to really grieve my mom and faced Mother's Day in a way I never had before. The day before Mother's day, my husband and sons took me to the beach. It was so sweet of them. They knew that it was a hard year, and they wanted to make Mother's Day and my birthday special.

Rebecca had a May birthday just like me and Debra, so I looked forward to possibly sharing it like I did with Debra, but we didn't have the same type of friendship. Debra and I were stay-at-home moms, and Rebecca and I were business owners with busy schedules. The week of our birthday was extremely busy with jobs for both Rebecca and me, and there was simply no time to celebrate. My birthday felt dark and lonely. Somehow, the universe had forgotten it was MY DAY.

My client that day was so sweet. It was the week she was moving in her home, and we didn't even have all her boxes unpacked, but she wanted to do something special for me. She baked a can of biscuits and stacked them up with a candle on top. That was my official birthday cake. That evening, Joe had a meeting and there was no time to celebrate. Charlie took me to the movie, but I really just wanted to go home and get the day over. Happy Birthday to me.

The following Monday I went to Rebecca's home to help her with an organizing project. When she came out of the room she said, "Let's go eat first." After we ate, she said, "Let's walk around Town Center." I never once guessed what the day was about. I thought she was stalling and just didn't want to organize. We went in this cute shop, and I found some fun things to buy. I decided to buy her a gift, but when I went to purchase something for myself she said, "Wait, aren't we supposed to buy gifts for each other? Isn't that what you and Debra did?" Oh my gosh! I felt so happy.

There were times when friendship with Rebecca was so difficult, and then there were days like this one, where she really came through. The universe (courtesy of Rebecca) finally remembered it was my birthday. It was most certainly a light in a very dark season.

Kevin's Story – M is for Murder

Kevin was a disarmingly charming and good-looking stockbroker. He was a divorced father of two children; an outgoing 14-year-old girl and a shy 10-year-old boy. "I want you to get all the closets and rooms in order because one day I think my kids will live with me," he said. After a month of organizing for him, I received a call from his assistant. "Kevin's ex-wife has been murdered. Can you come and help?"

I had only briefly met Kevin's ex-wife. She was tall, slender, and beautiful. Her skin was fair and her mannerism very soft and genteel. She shook my hand lightly, but with a big smile. Her funeral was standing room only as people made their way to say their goodbyes. "How can someone that seemed so well liked, be murdered?" I thought.

They suspected the murderer had been someone she trusted, and later it was revealed that her boyfriend had taken her life. That one day I briefly met her, had I known it would be her last day, I may have said something different to her than just to exchange casual pleasantries. I was glad to be a part of getting Kevin's home in order and then be there to support the family during a difficult time.

Chapter Eighteen
WHEN THE PAST COMES TO VISIT

May of the same year, I was at the home of a friend for a crawfish boil. As one of her friends and I were chatting, her friend asked, "Where are you from?" I get that in Houston a lot, you know, people hear my accent and want to know where I am from. I said, "I am from New Orleans." She asked me what part of New Orleans I was from and I said, "When I was little, I lived in Lakeview." With each of my answers to each of her questions, she seemed more and more excited. She asked me, "What street in Lakeview?" When I answered, "General Haig Street," the pitch of her voice became noticeably higher, "What was your house number?"

At that point, I became startled and said, "I'm sorry. Who are you?" Turns out, she was my next-door neighbor on General Haig Street in Lakeview, when I was a small child. Her family was the family I played with as a little girl. It seemed surreal. I went home and got the picture that I had recently found of me in front of her home with her sisters. I sent a text of the pictures to her and to my friend. We couldn't believe it. There were so many memories from my past surfacing during that time, so it was crazy that a real live person from my past was sitting in front of me. I felt like it was a reminder from God that there had been happy moments in my past.

Our mind and memories are interesting things. When I was a young teenager, I often told my mom about things I remembered as a little girl. She would look at me oddly and say, "Lisa, that didn't happen. You're imagining things." One day, mom was standing across the street talking to a neighbor when I overheard her say, "Lisa remembers more than I care she did." I tucked that comment away. Somehow, I knew that was important information.

After mom died, my brother, Andy, disappeared from the family for 11 years. He went back to college and didn't communicate with our family. The only reason we knew anything was because he stayed in contact with his ex-wife and only daughter. One day, not too long before Hurricane Katrina hit, he called to say he was visiting in Houston and would love us to meet someone. Joe and I met him and his new fiancée at a local restaurant. After dinner, we walked out to the parking lot, Andy and I walking a little ahead of Joe and Andy's fiancée. Andy proceeded to tell me all the things he remembered growing up, things that had driven him to separate himself from the family.

I became ill. My stomach was convulsing, and I had chills. Everything I remembered and was told didn't happen, did. Here was my brother confirming it all. We had been abused as children, both physically and emotionally by the hands of our parents and some of the relatives. "Remember when you were depressed and hospitalized, mom and dad were so embarrassed," Andy said. "They also said you were sexually promiscuous." he continued. "Why was going out with different guys wrong? I was just having fun and enjoying myself. They were my friends!" I cried. I had become the symbol that our family was not perfect. It was very difficult to hear. As we parted ways, I felt like a caged animal desperately needing to be freed and to run away.

"This year has been too much for me to process. I need a break from my own life," I thought.

Raquel's Story – My Wife, My Life

I answered the phone one day to a woman sobbing. "Do you help people unpack and organize?" She asked. "Yes ma'am," I replied. "May I ask you a few questions?" I continued. I have a standard list of questions that I ask my clients that assist me in knowing a little more about them and how I can help them better. No two people have the same situation. It's important to get to the big picture.

Raquel explained to me that she was recently divorced with custody of her twin daughters. "I moved to this side of town to be close to my mom, but I feel I have lost my friends as well," she cried. Once again, I knew I could relate.

At my first appointment, I met Raquel still in her pajamas, grieving her divorce. Her hair was unbrushed, and she was trembling. "I am a nervous wreck. I can't believe my wife would do this to me," she said. I wasn't quite prepared to hear all the information that she shared. She continued by saying, "I'm afraid of what this is doing to my children." Raquel was of a different faith, but I happened to notice a Children's Bible in the living room. I wasn't sure what made me say it, but I looked at her and replied, "Are you reading the Word of God to them?" Her response surprised me. She said, "No, I should though. Someone just gave my girls that Bible. Would you pray for me?"

It's in these moments, I love what I do. Not just organizing a room, but making a difference in someone's life, by guiding them to get organized on the inside.

Uncluttering our lives isn't just about organizing the rooms in our house. It's about uncluttering our lives, inside and out.

Chapter Nineteen
CHANGE THE SCENERY

G rowing up, my mom periodically rearranged the furniture. She moved the sofa from the wall by the kitchen to the area perpendicular to the front door. It gave the allusion of an entryway. This habit of hers absolutely drove my dad crazy. He worked the evening shift, and one night he came home around 1:00 a.m. completely clueless that he was about to be upended, literally. As he walked into the house, the newly formed "entryway" (aka the sofa) stopped him dead in his tracks. When his body, in full forward motion, met with the resistance of the sofa, he literally flipped head over feet, landing with a thud on the other side of the sofa. It's a funny picture now, but keeping in mind I come from a fiery, Italian family, you can imagine the uproar in our house that night!

And you'd think she'd learn, but just when dad got used to the new arrangement, mom would move it again. Moving the furniture around made mom feel better about our small home. She thought it would create a better flow. Space was space and something we didn't have a lot of.

Later in life, when things felt stressful to me, or I needed to concentrate on some writing or office project, I rearranged the décor on my walls or cleaned out a closet or cabinet. Joe didn't let me move furniture, so I'd just buy or rearrange the decor. For some reason changing the scenery and organizing felt like it calmed the chaos, and I could be productive.

"Rearrange the scenery," I thought to myself once in the midst of redecorating. "Rearrange the scenery and things will be better." And that's just what I did.

I had reconnected with my cousin, Anne, on Facebook; she was living in the idealistic town of Woodstock, Vermont, and had invited me to visit. "That's it!" I thought. "I will go to Vermont and come back and things will be better." Vermont was absolutely beautiful with the green mountains and the quaint shops in the small downtown. It was like a picture out of a magazine.

Anne was my mom's cousin and close friend. They were close in age. She had also lived in half of the double across the street from Grandma and Grandpa Buccola in Lakeview. She knew the family that I just connected with at my friend's home in Houston. I talked to Anne about all the inner distress that I felt I was dealing with and she gave me a book to read. "Maybe you need to make peace with your mom," she said. Well that was the understatement of the century!

The book was about how women deal with the loss of a mother. I eerily saw myself in the pages of the book. Even though I thought I made peace with the death of my mom, it was still a void to not have her, and I still felt angry with her for things that happened as a child. At the time of my visit there, Anne was also writing a book. As I read her manuscript, it was as if we had the same story. Of course we had the same story, we are cousins, and she lived with us. I began to write my thoughts and felt better.

The next day I was ready to conquer the world. We went into town to visit all the cute little shops. I loved the small town; even the pets were welcomed in the shops. It was the most awesome feeling. We could actually park our car and walk all around town on brick roads. Imagine not having to fight traffic. I enjoyed looking at the white picket fences around the houses and watching the young women push their babies around in strollers. That evening ended perfectly with Anne fixing grandma's recipe for Beef Braciole.

By morning, I don't know what triggered the conversation, but as I sat and talked with Anne, I wept bitterly once again. I shared with her all my feelings of abandonment; mom dying, dad remarrying right away and then my mom's sibling who had pledged to be the grandparent of my sons and care for us, but through some disagreement, I am not clear why, ceased communication with me. I felt abandoned by her as well.

I realized that becoming friends with Debra after mom's death had filled in all those empty places. So when Debra died, I just put up walls, and felt I lost a whole family. In truth, I felt abandoned by Debra as well.

I spoke to Anne about how I felt about our messy home growing up, and the relationship I had with my mom. Anne said, "Lisa, your mom was overwhelmed. She had four children in six years by the time she was 23-years-old." She continued by saying, "I know she wasn't touchy-feely and didn't give you the physical affection you needed, but none of the women in our family were touchy-feely. Your mom lived out what she knew."

The time with Anne was an opportunity to ask questions I had about my mom and my past. I was able to get some resolve, kind of like decluttering my thoughts. In the same sense, I thought about all my clients who think if they rearrange the piles of clutter and buy the cute containers then things will be better. The truth is, we have to clean out the clutter in our heart and minds, and I had some serious cleaning out to do in mine.

Organizing and rearranging gives a sense of newness and a fresh beginning. But we can't just stuff things in cute containers and call it organized. A huge part of organizing is purging. Sometimes people aren't ready to go through everything and purge. Rearranging is much easier. Buying a pretty, new container feels good and temporarily hides the clutter in our lives. It gives us a feeling that things are new and better. But at some point, we need to get rid of junk in our lives and create new habits, not just repackage them.

As I sat there thinking about my clients and what I had learned watching them declutter their lives, I thought, "Wow...I need to clean up my heart and head. I need to face these painful memories and forgive others," I thought. It was very difficult though. In no way do I want you to think this was an easy process. But I couldn't just continue to rearrange the broken pieces of my life. I needed to face my past if I had any chance at a healthy future.

Mary's Story – You Can't Have It All

Mary was an absolutely precious and positive woman, but she was very physically ill.

She walked around her home very slowly with a tube in her nose. An immune disorder had attacked her respiratory system, and as a result, she was unable to care for her home and children. "My husband works full time and is not very organized," she explained. "He can barely care for our boys, much less our home," she laughed.

Mary's home was a mess, but she had a tremendous support system that helped her in other ways. Her parents went to the grocery store for her. Mary also had a housekeeper. Through all she was going through, she felt so blessed to be surrounded by loving and caring friends and family. Financially she didn't have a care in the world; oil investments had brought in a substantial income to their household.

Each time I left from organizing, I was met with conflicting feelings. I was glad to help, but felt sad about her health, and as time had passed, her condition deteriorated. As of this writing, she is waiting for a transplant.

Just recently another client lost her battle to cancer. Like Mary, loving family and friends also surrounded her. It is hard for me to get close to someone and then they die, but it really puts things in perspective for me. For both these women had all the money in the world and an incredible family, but that did not insure them a long, healthy life.

It's easy to believe that if you have a loving family and material possessions that your life will be easy, but that simply isn't true. We strive so hard in this world for things. We want the love of others. We want health and a long life. But none of us can have everything.

Knowing these two women taught me to be grateful for the good things I have in this world, no matter what those good things may be.

Chapter Twenty
COMING UNRAVELED

Coming home from Vermont was not the end of my turmoil. I was still plagued with unsettled emotions about Mom, Debra, and my friendship with Rebecca. There seemed to be a connection between my feelings about Mom, the loss of Debra and my relationship with Rebecca, but I had no idea what the connection was. As I sat on the plane, my thoughts going a million different directions, I noticed a tiny thread in the sweater I was wearing. I pulled it ever so gently, obviously not wanting to make a hole. At first, the thread moved gently, but as I realized I was making it worse, I tried tightening my grip on the thread in order to snap it off. But the stupid thread wouldn't break. My frustration must have been incredibly evident because the woman sitting next to me, an older woman, probably in her mid-to-late eighties, put her hand over my hand that was pulling the thread. She didn't speak, but looked into my eyes questioningly and held up a pair of nail clippers. I nodded my approval, and she clipped the thread. Looking down, I realized I had pulled that loose thread until it had become a gaping hole. For some reason, I started to cry, realizing that just like my sweater, I was becoming unraveled, and all my efforts at fixing the problem were just making it worse.

I began to lose interest in my business, church, and other things I used to hold dear. I was spending money recklessly, and I began drinking. It's easy to drink when the people you are hanging out with are also drinking. Growing up, drinking was taboo and was associated with bad people who were going straight to hell.

I remember when I first moved to Houston I saw a dishtowel in a Texas boutique that said, "I love Jesus and I drink a little." I laughed pretty hard at that, but there was a lot of truth in that dishtowel, at least as it related to the people I was doing life with in Houston. The people I hung out with all loved God, and the majority of them drank. That was my excuse. They drank, so I drank. I loved the giddy feeling that came with drinking, but my drinking went from being something I did socially to something I did to escape. Shopping became another problem as well, another avenue of escape. Funny how buying something new gives you a short euphoric feeling, but leaves you empty, guilty, and with extra clutter.

I came home from Vermont and as I sat and had lunch with Rebecca, I shared with her all that was going on. Rebecca told me I needed to talk to a professional, but I guess deep down I knew I was out of control, because I had already made the appointment. The day of the appointment I sent a text to Rebecca and said, "I don't know if I can do this and go to the appointment. Maybe if I stay in bed, this will all go away." But she was having none of it. She said, "No, go, don't wear makeup and let yourself cry. If you pretend you are strong you will just waste your time."

That first appointment opened all kinds of memories of my mom and my childhood. It was such an emotional appointment that when I left, I couldn't bear to think about any of it. By the second appointment, I was ready though, and even had a list of things to talk about. (The great thing about being a professional unclutterer is that once I determine the problem, I make a list!) The counselor's office called and said, "Mrs. Giesler, we are so sorry, but we are going to have to reschedule your appointment; the therapist has hurt her back."

"Are you kidding?" I exclaimed! "I need to talk to someone! I have a list!"

"I'm sorry," said the office assistant, "but you can only talk to another therapist if you want to officially change therapists."

Well I certainly didn't want to start over with a new therapist, so I really had no choice but to wait another week. That week was grueling and wreaked havoc on my emotions. I felt like I had fallen and could barely get out of the bed. My doctor had given me a prescription for an antidepressant a couple of months earlier that I had not started taking. My sister recommended that I began taking the antidepressant, which I did. She sat with me that whole first day; my husband took off work and sat with me the second day. My oldest son, JoJo, took me on errands and cared for me the third day. And then somewhere on the fourth day, I got on my computer and made a checklist of all the things that I had let get out of hand the past month.

A little at a time, I began to take care of things around the house and the business. The following week my younger son, Charlie, graduated from his two-year internship and started working for me full-time. It felt good to have someone with me to keep me moving during such a difficult time. But I was far from okay.

Susan's Story – I'm a Mess Again

Susan was a quiet and mild mannered woman. She had a warm, but sad smile. "Lisa I have decided that this is the year to get organized and start taking better care of myself," she said. Susan faced a lot of disappointments the year prior. She had been laid off from a starter company. "It wasn't just the fact I had been laid off, but I helped start the company with a mutual friend who was a man. He then turned and gave away my position to a man who wasn't qualified. I feel betrayed. I hate men and the good ole boy club. My ex-husband was the same way," she said.

Knowing there is always a story behind the mess, I was not surprised by the rest of Susan's story. "After that I sunk into a depression and felt like 'what's the use in trying,'" she continued. Susan finished by saying, "But it's time, Lisa. It's time to get up, dust off, get back into life, and I need someone to hold me accountable."

Each time I came to organize with Susan, she began to brighten up. By the end of the first year, she was making great progress. At times Susan would call and say, "Lisa I have a mess again." I always assured her by saying, "That's ok. We'll take care of it and have fun visiting." The light returned to her eyes, and she felt optimistic about the future. It felt really nice making a difference in her life.

Chapter Twenty-One

MY CLOSET IS EMPTY; MY ROOM IS A MESS

I couldn't think straight. They say when all the neurotransmitters in your head get out of whack; sometimes medication is the only way to reset things. I think I waited so long to take medication though, because somehow in my mind, taking medication meant I was weak. I still remembered my mom's words in my ears when I had taken anti-depressants as a young adult. "Lisa, those pills make you look stupid."

But I want women to be okay getting the help they need, even if that help is medication. I think of it like this, if your immune system is down and you get sick, you need an antibiotic and rest to get better. Take your vitamins, eat well, and rest. The same is true of mental illness (yes, depression is a mental illness). You need the help you need. It might be medication, it might be counseling, it will most certainly require rest, and it might be a combination of all three.

Once I started taking my medication and getting the counseling and the rest I needed, I started trying to uncover how all this had started. Was it menopause that had caused my sudden upheaval of emotions? And why had my new friend, Rebecca, been the trigger to processing past memories that I needed to address? Even as I write, this I am concerned about what others will think. I'm not blaming anyone for anything, I'm just in the process of uncluttering, and that requires very real and very honest self-evaluation.

It feels much the same as when I am helping someone organize a closet. We drag everything out to sort and purge. It looks worse and is messy before it looks better. Right now, I feel my closet is empty, but my room is a mess. I need to get my thoughts sorted, purged, and organized. If all things work together for the good as the Bible says, then this will eventually help me to help others.

Cynthia's Story – Erasing Memories

Cynthia called me very desperately. She was a single mom with a growing business, but she felt stuck. "My home is disorganized, and it causes me to feel distracted," she said on the phone. As I sat with her for our first appointment, she told me she had five children ages six to nineteen years old. Most of them were sitting in the living room with us taking turns playing video games. I could understand her stress in having so many children to raise alone.

In a situation like this, I knew that organizing one time was not the long-term solution to her situation. Cynthia was a very busy lady; in addition to her business were all of the school activities, homework, and grocery shopping. I presented the idea of showing her how she could have her children help her. She was open to setting up a schedule of chores for her children.

The first area she wanted organized was the master bedroom. Usually businesswomen want the home office organized, so I was a little taken back by her decision to start in her bedroom. As we began sorting through paperwork, books, clothes, toys, and miscellaneous items that had found their way into her bedroom, she stopped and held one item and began to cry. "He used to beat me, you know. I thought it was my fault and tried to stay together for the sake of the children. But one day he tried to kill me, and my children called the police on him."

I wasn't shocked by her revelation; I rarely am surprised anymore, and it gave me a little insight as to why she wanted to start in her bedroom. She continued by saying, "I feel like a failure as a parent for not being able to stay married. And I feel guilty about asking my children to help me with the house, Lisa." I told her there was no way she could run a business and take care of everything. I also told her what had happened to her wasn't her fault, and it didn't make her a bad mom.

Cynthia just needed someone to tell her she was ok and to give her permission to ask the children for help. We sorted and purged items and even rearranged her bedroom furniture (a skill I definitely learned from my momma!) With a house full of children, she needed a place of refuge for herself and she wanted to erase the memories of abuse from the room.

Chapter Twenty-Two
AT ARM'S LENGTH

Towards the end of June, I began having nightmares and flashbacks. As I left my second appointment with the therapist, I began to hear a flashback in my mind. It was of me yelling.

"Great," I thought, "Now I'm hearing voices too!" Humor has always been a release valve for me, so I guess I should be grateful I could laugh at myself a little, but in truth, it was very startling.

A few days later, I had a nightmare about my mom. In the dream, she was being critical and mean, and I was yelling at her to stop treating me so mean. Joe woke me because I was yelling in my sleep. The second night, I had a similar dream; only this time it was a friend being mean and critical. As I began to yell at her to stop being mean and to be nice, all of a sudden it was no longer her, but my mom. I woke up sobbing. It was a Sunday morning and I told Joe, "I am not going to church. You can go, but I am staying home." Joe said, "Lisa, I'm not going anywhere. I'm staying with you."

I felt ill emotionally. I was beyond overwhelmed, beyond trying to hold it all together. I said to Joe, "The boys are almost 23 and 25. It is time for them to know what is going on in my life." Joe called our sons into the room. Together, we shared the turmoils, struggles, and constant guilt and abuse I had endured in childhood and adulthood, as well as the backstory to my life. I sobbed so deeply, in part because I think it felt good to be real with them. I always wanted to look like a supermom. Anytime I did something "wrong" as a parent, I apologized profusely and joked with the boys saying, "I don't want you to end up in therapy as an adult." Of course we all laughed, but deep down I was serious.

It was a powerful time of communicating and healing with our sons. JoJo and Charlie both shared their own pains. My falling apart gave them the opportunity to open up like they never had before. That was a turning point for JoJo. As long as he thought his brother and I were perfect, he felt he couldn't relate. And it was also the first time in a long time that Joe had stepped up spiritually. I guess as long as I was in charge, (which was all the time) Joe didn't need to be the head. He was now taking the role, and it felt good to release it to him. The only thing I needed to hold onto anymore was my husband's and my sons' love for me.

One evening, Joe was on the computer. My moods had settled down a bit, but I still felt rocky at times. As I watched him work on his computer, I said, almost in a whisper, "Joe, I don't feel this is over yet, but I do know when it's over, I won't ever be the same again. You can't go through what I have gone through and go back to business as usual. I have had a mind shift." Joe got up from his computer and walked over to where I sat huddled in my chair. He hugged me reassuringly and said, "Lisa, it's ok. You don't have to be strong for me."

I still worried about how all this was affecting my sons and others, though. I mean, I was Lisa the Professional Organizer. I was supposed to have it all together, right? But I was anything but "together." I always tell my clients that you can't just rearrange, you have to purge if you want to truly organize your life. Well let me tell you, I was in the middle of the biggest purge in my life and there was nothing about it that felt great.

I think the biggest struggle of all was my relationship with God. Deep down, I knew I was angry with him. Angry for not giving me a better mom, angry for taking Debra, and yes, even angry for replacing them both with Rebecca. For goodness sake, I was a minister and here I was angry with the very God who had called me to this ministry. I had no idea how I was going to reconnect with Him, so I just went through the motions, following the rules of what I knew and keeping Him at arm's length while I wrestled.

I always had the tendency to be legalistic as it related to anything to do with God. My views and rules of Christianity had been very strict, mostly due to the way I was raised. I was a very black and white person and now things felt grey. I had to trust God and show my sons that I still loved God and knew He was still taking care of us, but like I said, I just wasn't sure how to get there. The following Sunday in church my pastor's wife, Renee', came looking for me. "Lisa," she said, "You have been on my heart and mind. How are you?" I told her I was better and that I would be traveling over the next month. It really wasn't a good time to discuss anything, but I appreciated the sincerity with which she asked.

One thing that had felt reassuring over the past several months was different friends from the church calling and texting me saying, "Hey Lisa, you've been on my mind; just checking on you." It felt as if God was saying, "I see you Lisa. I'm giving you your space, but I want you to know, I'm right here waiting for you, ready for when you want to let me closer than arm's length."

Karen's Story – Letting Go

Karen was a very shy and polite woman with a voice that was very soft and timid. She lived in a large beautiful home in the suburbs, a home she shared alone with her husband. Karen was a retired empty nester with grown children living in different states, and she had recently lost both of her parents.

She first called me to help her transition all of her office supplies back to her home after her retirement, and then to disburse her dad things. There were many things to go through and she was not ready to get rid of anything, a common response when children lose a parent. Additionally, Karen was ready to embrace her empty nest years and wanted to reorganize her home, but Karen's adult children did not want to part with their things, as well. They loved coming to visit and seeing their room in the exact way they had left it. It was like walking into a time warp.

This was definitely a challenge for me. I was dealing with three generations and six people with their vast collections of things. Karen was to be the only voice in this reorganization, but she was very overwhelmed, both wanting to move forward, but at the same time, hold onto the past and the memories held in the things they had accumulated over the years.

There were so many memories to go through and so many useful things that could be repurposed. The downsizing and organizing process took well over a year. Part of the process was allowing Karen to talk through the memories and the logic of keeping or not keeping. It was therapeutic to have someone that would not judge her or to be critical. It was also something that was very emotional and couldn't be hurried. The house was full, but so was her heart and mind with all the memories. She felt like if she threw something away, she was throwing the person away. I had to assure her she was not.

There were also moments where I would touch the item for her because for Karen to touch it only personified it. After she made peace with the fact that there was not enough room to keep everything, then it was important for her to feel that everything was either recycled or had a good home. We found good homes for many items. Some items went to poor families, retirement communities, and women in tough life situations.

Little by little, I watched her home become uncluttered. She chose only the best items to enjoy. She realized if you have too much, you don't even remember you have it. If you can't remember or see it, then you can't use it. If you can't use it, then you don't need to have it.

At the end of the process Karen said, "I feel happier and so much lighter. Thank you Lisa, you have been wonderful and patient."

Uncluttering takes time and patience. But the result is worth every moment of the process.

Chapter Twenty-Three

DREAM VACATION IN EUROPE

By August, just a few days before the trip to Europe, I began to feel a little more grounded and confident. Possibly, I was so busy and didn't really have time to think or worry about the things that had been going on. Being on the other side of the world and having limited contact from home and business responsibilities was relaxing. On our first stop, Joe and I visited dear friends in Belfast, Northern Ireland. The weather was perfect, and I enjoyed touring the old castles. Our next stop was in Rome. Rome is a city rich with history, and I was in awe at the Vatican, St. Peter's Basilica, and the Pope's Cathedral. It was an inspirational experience. I was so awed and moved by the presence of God. I felt connected to Him there. I had never gone to confession, but I did in Italy. I felt it was the right thing to do, and in some way, it connected me to my Italian Catholic roots. Joe and I then took the Eastern Mediterranean cruise; it was the best. One of the stops included Sicily and visiting other sites and other cathedrals. My favorite stop was in Turkey. I visited the home of the Virgin Mary and the ruins in Ephesus, which included seeing the theatre where the apostle Paul preached, the senate seat, the library, and the road where Anthony and Cleopatra rode on; the whole trip was amazing. To be where the church began, it made everything in the Bible and history become so real.

On many of the afternoons, I found myself relaxing by the pool and people watching. Observing all the sunbathing bodies made me think about the vanities that people struggle with. We think if we have the perfect body, perfect house, or the perfect trip, then we will be happy, but it is not true. I was a woman who loved to talk, with a husband who didn't talk much, on a ship and in countries where few spoke English. I was on the perfect vacation, yet at times it felt lonely. I seriously needed girl time for chatting. My solution was an all too familiar friend at the time, drinking. I drank heavily. It numbed the thoughts and made me laugh.

When I was a young girl, whenever I felt down about things I disappeared into a made up world. Anything I needed or wanted; I just imagined. I imagined living in a world where I was loved unconditionally. I also imagined myself being bold and confronting those people who were ugly to me. I set up scenarios, played them out in my head, and it would soothe me. While laying on the ship, drinking myself into a numbed oblivion, I found myself going into pretend worlds again. But then I would have these epiphany moments that would snap me out of it. "What are you doing, Lisa, and who are you becoming?" I would think to myself. I also began to feel I was no longer qualified as a minister. I didn't feel my life was right. I still loved God and I still relied on praise and worship music. The music was like a prayer that had the words I didn't feel I had. But the irony of it all was that for the first time in my life, I was not being nagged by guilt.

How could I have made such a drastic change in my view of religion and my behavior? I had always been a narrow minded, black and white person. Either it was right or wrong, no grey areas. I had been so far to the right and now I was swinging towards the left. What I needed was to find my center.

After I came home from Europe, I was anxious to visit with Rebecca and get into the rhythm of things. She had helped me work on a couple of projects while I was gone and wanted to catch up and have girl talk. I seriously underestimated the effects of jet lag. There was so much to do, and I was so overwhelmed, but I am usually in go mode, so I said yes. Rebecca and I decided to go to lunch at a sandwich shop near her business. We took her car and left mine at her store, giving us more time for chatting on the way! At lunch, the conversation started off casual, and I am not sure how, but it switched to talking about my mom and the abuse that happened growing up.

As Rebecca and I talked, I told her of the years of verbal and physical abuse I had suffered at the hands of my father. As we talked, I had a sudden memory of being a young girl playing in my backyard with a neighborhood teen. He pushed me down on the ground and tore my panties. I shared with her about the sexual abuse I had endured as a very young little girl at the hands of that teen, abuse that my mom knew about but brushed off as nothing.

I was not prepared for the next statement that came from Rebecca's mouth. "Do you think you are angry with your mom for not protecting you?" she asked. I jumped from my chair and said, "I'm done, I can't talk about this!" and walked out of the restaurant. I felt like I had been punched in the stomach and the wind had been knocked out of me. I couldn't think.

The reality hit me that I was not in my vehicle. I looked down at my heels and tried to figure out if I could walk the city blocks back to where my vehicle was parked. Rebecca came outside and unlocked her vehicle. She got in and sat in the driver's seat while I wrestled with whether or not I wanted to get in. When I finally made a decision and got in, I sat there and stared out the window, I couldn't speak. A few minutes later she said, "I'm sorry for crossing a line, Lisa."

By the time we returned to her business, Rebecca was crying. We exchanged hugs and lightly joked about raccoon eyes. Crying and mascara don't mix. Later on, I sent her a text that simply said, "Thank you for lunch." She replied back, "No, thank you." She had clearly hit a nerve, and all I wanted to do was get in bed and have a good cry.

The odd thing was, I never had a problem talking about things with Rebecca or with Joe, but this was different. I wasn't sure what exactly happened and what had triggered that buried memory, but I definitely wasn't ready to address it.

When I am in the process of uncluttering and organizing a client's home, I so often hear them say, "Wow, I forgot that was even in there!" So many times in the process of purging and getting our lives together, we discover something that we had forgotten was there. This was one of those moments.

Danette's Story – Controlling Something, Anything

Danette was a 55-year-old woman in great physical shape. I always envied those whose genetics were on their side. I also admire the discipline of a woman who exercises daily. I guess one day I may find that time in my schedule.

Danette asked me to help her organize her closet. I walked into her home. It was beautifully decorated and appeared organized. Her closet showed minimal disorganization, but had a lot of hidden clutter. As we began to organize, she said, "I know this is a small job, and I should be able to do this myself, but it feels overwhelming. I really need someone to talk to. She continued, "My husband hardly notices me. I had plastic surgery three months ago, and he has not once even acknowledged it."

The story always comes out. I never know when it will make its appearance, but I am never surprised when it arrives.

Once Danette's closet was finished, she said to me, "Lisa, in the mornings, having an organized closet and being able to pick out my clothes with ease gives me an area of order that I can control. I can't control my marriage, but I can handle my wardrobe. Thanks."

As I left, I gave her a hug goodbye. She needed to know that someone cared. Sometimes, in the midst of our clutter, (however minimal it may seem to others), we become lost and overwhelmed and just need someone to help us find our way.

Chapter Twenty-Four
A VISIT FROM THE GRAVE

A few Sundays later, Joe and I were at another couple's home, Bobby and Sonya, watching the preseason football games. It was the New Orleans Saints versus the Houston Texans, (for the record the Saints won that day) and was such a fun day. After lunch, Sonya and I took a walk around the neighborhood, despite the sweltering summer heat and humidity. As we walked, we talked and caught up on life. I told her about a lot of the junk in my head.

For the first time, I opened up about my friendship with Rebecca. I told her how much I wanted and needed from Rebecca and how frustrated I was that she was often not there for me in the ways that I needed her. I told her the thoughts I had about feeling that my relationship with Rebecca was somehow connected to my struggle with my mom and my friendship with Debra.

Very honestly and with great care she said, "Lisa, you couldn't control who your mom was and your relationship with her, and you couldn't control Debra's death, so stop trying to control your friendship with Rebecca. Stop expecting so much from her and just enjoy the good times you have with her." How simple. How profound. She said, "You need to let go of the hurt and the pain of your past."

The next day my boys returned home from a weekend in New Orleans. JoJo had turned 25 and he and Charlie went to celebrate with their childhood friends, Seth and Joel. The boys didn't return alone, but they had Seth and Joel with them. It was such a treat and so good to see them. When I saw Seth walk through the door, I became so emotional. Seth, Debra's son, was standing in my door. It was like a visit from the grave.

The last day Seth was at the house before they headed home, we sat in the living room, and I shared Debra stories with him.

He was older and wouldn't have remembered all the things that happened. I wanted him to know who his momma was as my friend. We laughed and cried. It felt so good and at the same time made me miss her all the more. I loved her so much. When Seth left, he told me that when he married, I would be the mother of the groom. What a sweet boy. What a sweet young man.

The day they left, I took them to meet Rebecca. I wanted her to meet Debra's son. She knew how much Debra meant to me, so it felt so good to see her meet Seth. It was like she was meeting Debra.

Linda's Story – By All Appearances

"If only...I was rich then my life would not be stressful" I heard a woman business owner say.

"Having money is not what it's cracked up to be," a housewife said to me. "My husband is awful, you know he beats me and cheats on me; I feel trapped. I have no money, and I'm not smart. Where would I go with my children?" I said, "Don't say that about yourself, you are a very smart woman; I'll help you come up with ideas for yourself. You should talk to someone at the women's shelter. They can guide you." I replied.

"If only... I was married, I wouldn't be lonely, and then my life would be complete." I heard a female law partner say.

"I thought he was the one, he was educated, romantic, and now he won't work, he won't go out with friends and he verbally abuses me. I would feel guilty if I left him. My kids would be devastated. They idolize him. I feel trapped," she said. "That's a decision only you can make, I'm not sure if I could stay," I replied.

If only...I had a big and pretty house like my sister. Funny thing is that in less than three months her sister confided that her husband had lost his bonus and she didn't know if they were going to lose their house. Life became a scramble for her sister to keep up appearances. Her sister's life was not what it seemed.

Many people are waiting for certain things to make their life better, but often those things, that perfect set of circumstances they are looking for, never come. They judge the lives of others, and by all appearances find them to be perfect, but rarely is that the case of anyone.

I met Linda at a business networking meeting. She was very tall, slender, and beautiful. Her personality was just as beautiful. I never saw her wear the same outfit twice. Linda was a sales rep for a pharmaceutical company and her husband was an engineer with an oil and gas company.

"My husband is building his dream home, and I need your help in getting ready for the move," she said. I was surprised at how her home looked. Since she was meticulously dressed and accessorized, I had imagined her home to look the same. We became fast friends as I helped her through the sorting, purging, and pre-boxing of her home. During the process, she confessed their money challenges. "It's all about image to him," she complained. "It feels overwhelming to try and keep up with the people at the country club. One night at supper at the club, my friend talked about one day getting a Mercedes. As we walked outside, the valet driver pulled up in a Mercedes. I was afraid to tell her it was mine, and when she realized it was, she was so mad and jealous that I got one first. My husband insisted I have one. If she only knew we were not as rich as it seems," she said.

I was glad to work with Linda. It helped her to relax; she didn't feel like she needed to impress me. At the end of the day, I think we all want someone to see through our façade so we can escape from it.

Chapter Twenty-Five
TRUTH REVEALED

On a warm Sunday evening in early September, I walked into my living room and was greeted by "Hello Sweetums, what'cha doing?" I replied, "I'm finished writing the book." But even as I said the words I thought in my head, "How can I be done? I don't feel better yet." For some reason, I thought writing a book would be the best way to unclutter my life. You know, get it all out there. Let the chips fall where they may. But I was wrong. Something was still very definitely hiding inside the closed off places in my mind. But not for long.

I wasn't sure why. Nothing bad had happened that day. But after pronouncing that my book was finished (which it obviously was not), I got up and walked around to pray. Suddenly, I began having memory flashes of myself being abused as a little girl. I could see the places and recognize my voice and the voices of some relatives. It was too much to handle. I cried for the next three hours and realized I needed to get some sleep because I needed to see clients that day.

I woke up in denial over all I had remembered, but the memory fit into the missing puzzle pieces of my life. Over the next couple of days, I called family members. I needed to verify a few things. The first person I called was Daddy. I asked him where I lived when Judy was born. He said I lived with Francis. I said, "What about when I got older Daddy?" And he said, "Lisa, you never lived with family in Lakeview." But I knew that wasn't right. I had very specific memories about being passed around between family members. Daddy worked the night shift, so maybe he didn't know I was being dropped off with other family all the time.

Then I asked him point blank, "Daddy why didn't momma like me and why didn't we get along?" I expected him to say

"Lisa, your momma loved you," but that is not what he said. He said, "Lisa, I got your momma pregnant when she was sixteen. She had a boyfriend who promised when she turned eighteen he would come back and get her and marry her, and that didn't happen. You were the reason she didn't have the life or the man she wanted, and she spent her life taking it out on you and me. She resented you for stealing the life she wanted, and I resented you for her misery." What a kick in the stomach.

That night I called one of my aunts. I asked, "Who took care of me when Judy was little and in the hospital?" "I did", she said. "Francis didn't want to deal with you and dirty diapers, so she passed you on to me." A few weeks later I talked with another relative and she said, "Do you remember Arty taking care of you?" He was a seventeen-year-old guy. What the heck, where were all the aunts to take care of me. Who loved me? Who was protecting me? Everyone I asked confirmed the reality I had lived with. I was unwanted, resented, rejected, abused, and abandoned at every turn throughout my life. It was sickening and difficult.

That Friday I shared the memories with my counselor. She said "Lisa you have to accept it happened and forgive." Accepting it would prove to be the first step. Over the following week, I found myself losing my grip. I yelled at my sons, and couldn't even let Charlie hug me. I then yelled at my bank manager for the identity theft that had been occurring. I was due to have an appointment with my pastor's wife and her assistant called to cancel. I yelled at her. I knew I needed an ear. I texted Rebecca and told her I needed her.

Once again, she rescheduled appointments to help me through my crisis. Rebecca and I always met at a certain coffee spot to chat. Kinda like our time to talk about family, business, and just basically decompress. We always picked a quiet spot. This one particular day, we sat outside, the weather was still warm, but the wind was blowing as I poured my heart out; I said, "I feel broken and don't see how I can keep helping others."

She reached across the table, grabbed my hand, and said "Lisa, you are a minister to others. Remember how you helped me?"

It was interesting to me the nature of my friendship with Rebecca. We were either great friends or just really seemed frustrated with one another (probably me more so than her). Every time she cancelled a meeting with me or didn't follow through with something she said she was going to do, the level of my irritation was irrational. And yet, at other times, like for my birthday, or dropping everything to come to my aid, she was the most incredible friend. I knew that I had walls around my heart, walls built by years of pain and distrust, and for some reason I wanted Rebecca both on the inside of those walls and firmly closed off on the outside of them.

I prayed I would someday understand the nature of our friendship.

Mattie's Story – An Outfit A Day

I arrived at Mattie's home in an exclusive part of the city. Mattie was very polite and very genteel. Her life was very busy assisting her husband in his business, helping her mom in her business, and trying to get her own business started. She introduced me to her children's nanny, who used to be her nanny as a child. Mattie proceeded to bring me upstairs to her problem area. The canopy on the bed was filled with clothes, with only a small opening for her husband to get in bed. At the foot of the bed were two laundry racks filled with clothes. The bookcase on the wall and the trunk were overflowing with clothes. On her bathroom floor was a pile approximately three feet high with clothes that needed to be cleaned. Her closet was cluttered with more designer clothes, shoes, purses, and miscellaneous items. The purging process was very difficult for Mattie.

At the end of our time, I counted how many outfits were still left. I said, "If you were to wear a different outfit each day for a year, you still have too many clothes." Her reply "I wear two different outfits a day." I left her home feeling like I had not made a difference. A year and a half later, I received a call from her. "Lisa, thank you so much for all that you did for me. As a result of what you taught me about organization, I was finally able to open my boutique and want to invite you to the grand opening."

You never know the impact organizing can make in a person's life.

Chapter Twenty-Six
PUSHING THROUGH

Less than a month after the brutal revelation my dad shared, I had a total knee replacement surgery. The night before surgery, I was a complete wreck. It wasn't just because of having surgery, which was part of it. I was afraid that people would forget about me; out of sight, out of mind. I was going to be out of commission for quite some time, and I was in such a fragile state at that point; so worried that people would abandon me. I was completely blessed at the number of women who came to visit, bring food, and coffee. They came to help me go to physical therapy or just to take me out when my sons were not available. I felt like it was God's way of telling me I mattered to people.

I knew with my head that recovery would be tough and a lot of pain, but I don't think it's something you can really prepare yourself for until you experience it. While I was in my bed recovering, I had an aha moment. My old knee needed to be removed and a new one put in, but healing doesn't happen by simply removing what is bad and putting in something new. There is the pain to push through. All the muscle and tendons must be put back together and then given time to adequately heal. And I couldn't just sit around dwelling on the pain either. I had to get up and be an active part of my own healing. I needed therapy and a great support system for my knee to heal.

The same was true of my emotional wounds. It wasn't enough that I was aware of the problem. I had to acknowledge and deal with all those old memories, and then allow the healing to take place as I pushed through the pain.

When Joe and I went to Europe, it was to celebrate 30 years of marriage and a time for just us. It had been quite a year for us as Joe watched me unravel and relive the abuse that had occurred as a child. He had compassion, but was confused and didn't know what to say. In his analytic and engineering world, he just wanted it logically fixed. Much like replacing an old knee with a new one. But just like my knee replacement, I was not going to be fixed overnight; I needed to process and push through the pain as though it just happened. To sweep it under the rug was not going to make it go away. I also needed to forgive and release those that had hurt and abused me.

The days following the nightmares in September, Joe sent me an email. In his email, he confessed for the first time how he had been feeling all those years, watching me struggle with my relationship with my parents and the resentment he felt. He thought for many years that I didn't respect him as a husband. He now saw that I wasn't trying to be against him, but I was caught in an abusive cycle. In his letter to me, he apologized for his behavior and promised to love and support me. I was so thankful for his willingness to humble himself and share those things with me.

I had everything I needed to heal.

A Common Story

A common thread that runs through the lives of many of the people that I organize is that they have more stuff than space. There are different reasons for that. One is the desire to have things we didn't have or needed as children. When many of us became adults, we made a decision to change that. That we would get what we thought we wanted or needed. For my husband, it was socks. We both came from families that didn't have a lot of money. He has a big drawer of socks because when he was younger he only had a few pairs. I see this in homes. A great majority of the things they think they wanted or needed is not being used. They may have used it once or twice. It occupies space, but it is difficult to get rid of it because of what it symbolizes. To say we no longer need it is hard to admit. It is much easier to say we will use it later, but later doesn't come. It is also difficult to release items because of the cost, but what is it really costing in space?

There is a benefit to purging and there is a benefit to keeping. The secret to uncluttering is knowing when to purge and when to keep.

Chapter Twenty-Seven

MAKING THE CONNECTION

While in recovery, I had a dream of an attic filled with things. Some were antiques and some just random boxes. In the corner of the attic, there was a ray of light coming through the attic window. On the floor, completely bathed in that light, was a small box. As I reached to pick up the box, two women appeared in front of me; my momma and Debra. When I saw them, I stepped backward, somewhat in fear and somewhat in surprise to see them there. As I stepped backward, I bumped into someone else and turned to see Rebecca standing there. She had such a calm look on her face as she pushed me toward them, encouraging me with each step that I took. And just as I reached them, they were gone and Rebecca stood in their place, holding the small box that had once been on the floor of the attic.

I realized (in my dream) that Rebecca had filled the void left both by my mother and by Debra. She represented the friendship I had with Debra and the critical, uncertain nature I had with my mother.

It's why I was always trying to make the connection between Rebecca and my mom and Debra. Rebecca caused me to face the rejections and feelings of abandonment I felt from both women and to make peace with my mom. She helped me to trust again.

When I reached for the box in her hand, she smiled at me and nodded, almost giving me permission to open the box. It was the most reassuring smile. I felt such strength and purpose as I opened the box. To my surprise, the box was completely empty.

I immediately knew it was my fresh start, an opportunity to store the memories I cherished and wanted to keep, and the room to make new memories.

Chapter Twenty-Eight
UNCLUTTERED AND STRONG

When I am working with a new client, I understand there is a process they must go through before they can let go. They must come to terms with their clutter, get over the fear of "what if I need that," realize they need help, and trust that I have their best interest at heart. Clutter can become a security that allows us to hide and not see what the real issue is.

Likewise, acknowledging the past and forgiving others are the first steps in making peace with your past. As I looked over the events of my life, the good with the bad, I wondered how I could have fond memories of a place and time that also caused so much pain. My pastor's wife said, "Lisa, good can exist with the bad in the picture of our lives. When the puzzle is all put together, then we can wrap it with a pretty bow." Once we understand why we do the things we do, it can make it easier to make the changes we need in our life.

Once we empty out the mess from our lives, we can't keep it empty. We must fill it with the right things. I get to decide what I will keep and what I will discard. Some of the painful memories, I will still keep to share and help others. And I will keep the precious memories of family and friendships that I cherish. I have found great strength in knowing I am in control of what I choose to hold onto and what I choose to let go.

no regrets. lessons learned. strength gained.
my faith has kept me.
~Lisa Giesler

Remember what I said in the Prologue, "No Regrets, Lessons Learned, Strength Gained, My Faith Has Kept Me?" I have no regrets. If I could rewrite my story, would I write it differently?

Of course. But I have learned great lessons from my life and have gained great strength as I uncluttered the chaos there. And through it all, my faith has been there to guide me, showing me the purpose God has given me in this world, to help others as they unclutter their own lives.

In the days when the chaos and clutter of your life threatens to overtake you, remember that God has given you a purpose on this earth. Your strength and purpose awaits you, even in the chaos and clutter. As you are ready to begin the process of uncluttering your life, choosing what you will keep and what you will let go, you will find great freedom.

Lisa's story, and the stories of her clients bring to light how a history with abuse or trauma of any kind change the way we view ourselves, others, the world *and in particular...* relationships. If as you read Lisa's book you felt a connection to the stories shared here I want you to understand how important it is for you to tell your own story. Shame is keeping you in the dark, and anything that tells you to hide is holding you hostage. Find a therapist you trust and tell your story. Allow the truth to be brought to light and live shame free. You will have guaranteed confidentiality with a therapist, who is trained to listen to you, and to walk with you on the journey to understanding the effects, the symptoms, and the damage to your core that trauma and abuse leave behind. While confiding in a close friend, family member, or confidant is often a first step, it can lead to those people taking on feelings of responsibility for your hurts because they want to help you, but may not know how.

Most survivors come to therapy thinking that although they have a history of abuse or trauma they've gotten over it, or it didn't have a lasting effect. Some come to therapy for other reasons and the history surfaces during an initial session. Either way, I implore you to avoid the dangers of self-help. Being your own therapist can lead away from recovery because if you are processing in an unhealthy or shaming way, there is nobody to offer another perspective or redirect your thoughts.

Chances are as a survivor your thought life is shaming and blaming. Ever had someone close to you say, "You're your own worst enemy." Well, that's because that other person sees how you shame and blame yourself. If you truly want to live to your full potential and make the most of every breath, then tell your story, fully and completely, to a professional, and unlock the hidden places that God is calling you to today. Shame is your worst enemy, and every human has been given the ability to overcome – take what is yours and live free! I will be praying for each of you.

Shannon E Strader MA, LPC

CPSIA information can be obtained at www.ICGtesting.com
Printed in the USA
LVOW07s1736090915

453466LV00006B/655/P